To
The
H

mama &
Papa xxx

Tayta's

Lebanese Kitchen

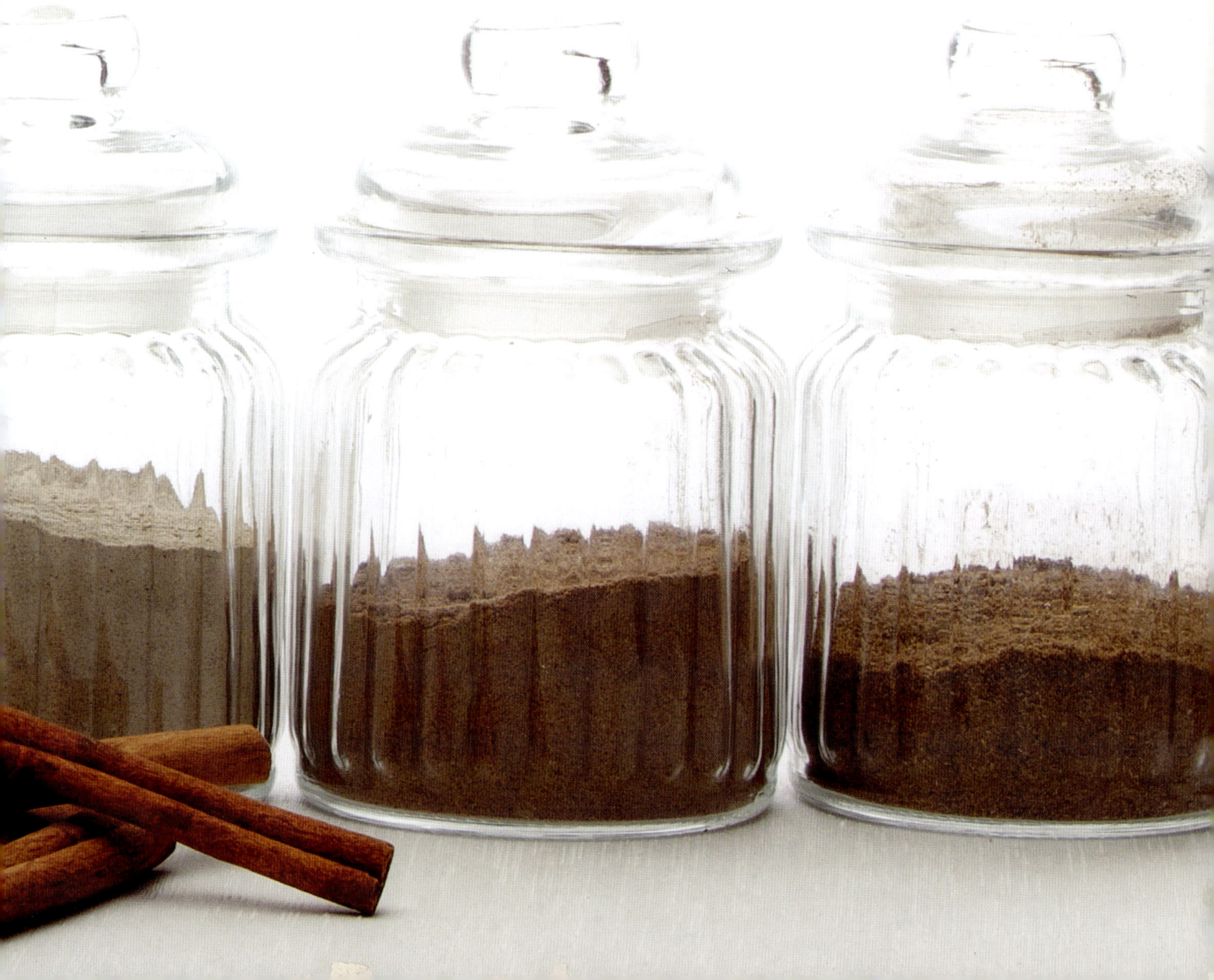

Tayta's
Lebanese Kitchen
Sue Dahman

To my beloved children.
I love you all so very much.

Recipe List

Tabbouli Salad (Tabbouleh)	11
Potato Salad (Salated batata)	12
Lebanese Mixed Spices	12
Salad with Croutons or Bread (Fattoush)	15
Hummus Salad (Salata el hummus)	16
Eggplant Salad (Salatat batingan)	19
Hummus (Hummus bi'tahini)	20
Baba Ghanouge (Baba ghanouge)	23
Garlic Paste (Taratour b'toum)	25
Yoghurt and Cucumber Dip (Khiyar b'laban)	25
Gnocchi Lebanese Style (Maakroon b'toum)	26
Meat Pizza (Lahme b'ajin)	31
Kafta Pizza (Lahme bil kobez)	32
Spinach Triangle (Fatayer spanech)	35
Pastry with Lamb (Sambousik)	36
Zaater Pizza (Manaheesh b'zaater)	38
Kibbee (plain) (Kibbeh)	41
Grilled Kibbee (Kibbeh ou'ras)	41
Baked Kibbee with Onion and Pine Nuts (Kibbeh b'sayneyeh)	43
Kibbee Balls (Kibbeh kebakib)	44
Kibbee Raw (Kibbeh nayye)	47
Kibbee Pumpkin (Kibbeh heeleh) vegetarian	49
Kibbee Fish (Kibbet el'samak)	50
Kafta Kebab (Kafta meshwy)	53
Kafta with Eggs (Kafta baayd)	54
Lamb Kebab (Lahme meshwy)	56
Garlic Chicken (Shish tawook)	57
Stuffed Rib and Lamb Shoulder (Dela'ah mehshi)	61
Pearl Couscous with Lamb and Chicken (Moghrabieh)	62
Okra with Rice (Bamia w'riz) vegetarian	65
Lebanese Rice (Riz b' sh'airieh)	65
Chicken and Rice (Riz ala'djaj)	66
Mouloukia (El mouloukia)	69
Cabbage Rolls (Mehshi malfouf)	70
Stuffed Zucchini (Mehshi kousa)	72
Stuffed Vine Leaves (Mehshi warak enib oteygh) vegetarian	75
Stuffed Silver Beet (Mehshi selek) vegetarian	77
Fish with Tahini (Samke harrah)	78
Grilled Fish (Samak meshwi)	80
Baked Fish with Walnuts (Samak bil'joz)	83
Lentil Soup or Monk Soup (Kibbet el'rahib) vegetarian	84
Mixed Legumes Soup (Maklouta) vegetarian	87
Lentils with Rice (Mjadra mdradrah) vegetarian	89
Green Beans with Oil (Loubia b'zaait) vegetarian	90
Falafel (El falafel) vegetarian	92
Fried Eggplant (Batingane maq'ley) vegetarian	94
Pan-fried Cauliflower (Arnabit maq'ley) vegetarian	95
Potato Wedges (Patata maq'ley) vegetarian	96
Semolina Biscuits with Walnuts (Ma'amoul)	101
Date Biscuits (Sewa)	102
Shortbread Biscuits (G'raibeh)	105
Aniseed Biscuits (Kaak)	106
Semolina Slices (Nammoura)	109
Baklava (Backlawi)	110
Pancakes with Walnuts or Cream (Katayef)	113
Doughnut Balls (Awamat)	115
Cream Slices (Ayesh el saraya)	116
Sweet Cheese (Halawat el jibin)	118
Lebanese Spicy Rice Pudding (Moghley)	123
Sweet Wheat (Snainiyeh)	124
Fig Conserve (Mar'abba el tin)	126

Introduction

I was born in the small village of Al Bouhaira, 'the lake', located in the north of Lebanon. The village is surrounded by mountains and is known for its agriculture – apples, pears, grapes, peaches and cherries. I have very strong childhood memories of the school holidays in summertime where the village was our playground. Not only did we play in the mountains but we would also gather with friends and my great-grandmother Maren, grandmother Zoumorod, mother Genevieve and other relatives to cook. The kitchen would be filled with big pots, making jams and preserves from the fruit of our trees – figs, pears, apricots and apples – and pickling olives, turnips, eggplant and vine leaves. We also made tomato paste and of course *arak*, the famous Lebanese drink. We gathered at different houses to do this, but mostly at my mother's house.

During the winter months we lived in our house in Tripoli, where we went to school. At lunchtime we would race home to the smell of my mother's cooking and I would try to guess what was on the menu as we climbed the stairs to our apartment. Our table was always busy at lunchtime, full of family and friends who would come to the city to visit the doctor or purchase goods to take back to the village. I can still hear the sound of my mother's voice: '*ahla wa sahla*' (you are welcome), she would say every time there was a knock on the door.

My father was a parish priest, *khouri*, and so my mother was well known and called the *khouriah*, which means priest's wife. During the Lent season, my mother would get up early and we would help her prepare and cook lunch to have after the church service when the priests and nuns would come to break bread and share a meal with us. My mother's kitchen was big – I remember the marble bench and the sink that we had to clean after every cook-off. I guess that's when I really developed my love for food and cooking.

As the years passed and I cooked for my own family and friends, I saw myself standing in my mother's shoes. As well as cooking many other dishes I still cook traditional Lebanese food, especially on feast days when I gather with my family, cousins and friends. On these days my children come early to help me prepare the food, just as I did with my own mother. And now my grandchildren call out, 'Tayta, can I taste some?' And they drag up a chair and stand by my side to help me cook. This gives me great pleasure and makes me more passionate about my love for cooking and my kitchen. I hope that my children will keep the feast days traditional also.

The Lebanese cuisine is abundant in fresh vegetables, fruit, fish and poultry along with beans and pulses, which are a rich source of vitamins. Lebanese bread is a staple part of our diet and is on the table with every meal. In the early days when we were living in the village, there was just one butcher and he killed a goat on Sunday after church, and everyone in the village bought a bit. That was the only meat we had until the following Sunday, as there was no refrigeration, so our diet was mainly fresh vegetables and legumes. Olive oil is used in nearly every meal, along with fresh herbs and spices. The freshness of the ingredients is very important.

It is faith, family and traditions that tie the Lebanese community together, including the preparation of delicious traditional food. Memories of my beloved mother have inspired my recipes and fruitful times in the kitchen. I am passionate about bringing the love of my family cooking and traditional Lebanese dishes to homes across Australia.

I have written this cookbook to keep my mother's recipes alive, and I hope to share all these wonderful family recipes with people who enjoy cooking and eating Lebanese food.

Sue Dahman, 2012

Tabbouli Salad
Tabbouleh

Tabbouli is one of Lebanon's most famous dishes and it is also a popular dish worldwide. Tabbouli is not only tasty but also good for you. It can be served as a mezza or a salad with barbecued meat.

Wash the burghul in cold water then drain and squeeze out any excess water. In a bowl combine the burghul, parsley, red onion, mint, spring onion, tomato and cucumber. Add the salt and black pepper and spices, then the olive oil and lemon juice. Mix well.

Serve with your favourite meat or cos lettuce.

Serves 4–6

¼ cup burghul (crushed wheat)

5 cups finely chopped flat-leaf parsley (about 2 bunches)

1 small red onion, finely chopped

handful finely chopped mint

3 spring onions, finely chopped

3 medium tomatoes, finely chopped

1 small Lebanese cucumber, roughly chopped

1 teaspoon salt, or to taste

½ teaspoon black pepper

½ teaspoon Lebanese mixed spices (see page 12)

¼ cup extra virgin olive oil

¼ cup lemon juice

Potato Salad

Salated batata

750g desiree potatoes

¼ cup extra virgin olive oil

½ cup chopped flat-leaf parsley

¼ cup finely chopped mint

½ cup finely chopped coriander

2 spring onions, finely chopped

½ teaspoon Lebanese mixed spices (see below)

1 teaspoon salt, or to taste

½ teaspoon freshly ground black pepper

juice of 1 lemon

Peel and quarter the potatoes. Boil them until tender then drain and cut into 3cm cubes. Place the warm potato in a serving bowl, drizzle with the olive oil and mix gently. Add the parsley, mint, coriander, spring onion, spices, salt, black pepper and lemon juice and toss gently to combine.

Serve warm or cold.

Serves 4–6

Lebanese Mixed Spices

¼ cup allspice berries

½ cup whole black peppercorns

2 teaspoons ground cinnamon

1 teaspoon ground nutmeg

I like to buy spices in small quantities so they are always fresh and store them in air-tight jars. You can mix your own or buy ready-made Lebanese spice mixes from Lebanese or Middle Eastern shops.

Use a spice grinder to grind the allspice and the peppercorns separately to a fine powder and mix together with the cinnamon and nutmeg. Store in a jar in a dark place. The spice mix will keep for 6 months.

Makes about 120g

Salad with Croutons or Bread
Fattoush

Bread was and still is treasured in Lebanon. It is seen as a blessing from God. If the bread is stale or cannot be used, it is kissed and thrown away along with an apology to the heavens for wastage. That is why we toast old bread and sometimes used it in fattoush. My mother use to say, 'We have some stale bread, we should make fattoush for lunch.' Alternatively, we sometimes fried the bread in vegetable oil and used it as crackers for dips such as hummus, baba ghanouge or labne (cream cheese).

For the dressing, combine all the ingredients in a small bowl and set aside.

Heat the vegetable oil in a small frying pan over high heat. Add one-third of the bread cubes and fry until golden brown. Remove with a slotted spoon and place on paper towel to drain. Repeat this step until all the bread is fried.

Combine all the vegetables and herbs in a bowl. Add the spices, drizzle over the dressing and mix well. Add the croutons and toss gently.

Serve immediately to enjoy the crunchy texture of the croutons.

Serves 4–6

1 cup vegetable oil

1 piece of Lebanese bread, cut into 3cm cubes (croutons)

1 Lebanese cucumber, cut in half lengthways and sliced

4 radishes, thinly sliced

3 medium tomatoes, coarsely chopped

2 cups coarsely chopped iceberg lettuce

4 spring onions, finely chopped on the diagonal

1 cup purslane (optional)

1 cup coarsely chopped flat-leaf parsley

½ cup coarsely chopped mint

2 teaspoons ground sumac

½ teaspoon freshly ground black pepper

½ teaspoon Lebanese mixed spices (see page 12)

DRESSING

1 teaspoon salt, or to taste

2 tablespoons lemon juice

¼ cup olive oil

Hummus Salad

Salata el hummus

1½ cups dried chickpeas

½ teaspoon bicarbonate of soda

½ cup finely chopped parsley

¼ cup finely chopped mint

2 medium tomatoes, chopped

2 spring onions, chopped

¼ teaspoon ground cumin

DRESSING

2 cloves garlic, crushed

½ teaspoon salt, or to taste

2 tablespoons lemon juice

¼ cup olive oil

For the dressing, place all the ingredients in a small bowl and mix well. Set aside.

Place the chickpeas and bicarbonate of soda in large saucepan and cover with water. Leave to soak overnight.

Drain the chickpeas and add 4 cups water. Bring to the boil over medium–high heat, then reduce the heat and simmer for 30 minutes, until the chickpeas are cooked, topping up the pan with cold water if necessary.

Drain the chickpeas and transfer them to a serving bowl. Add the parsley, mint, tomato, spring onion and cumin, drizzle over the dressing and mix well.

Serve with your favourite meat or with dry crunchy Lebanese bread as a mezza.

NOTE: If you don't have time to prepare your own chickpeas, substitute 2 cans of chickpeas, drained and rinsed.

Serves 4

Eggplant Salad

Salatat batingan

For the dressing, place all the ingredients in a small bowl and mix well. Set aside.

Pierce the eggplants with a fork in about 4 places then chargrill on a gas stove until soft, turning regularly. Alternatively, you can microwave them on high for 15 minutes, or bake in the oven at 200°C for 40 minutes, until tender.

Plunge the eggplants in cold water and remove the skin, then chop the flesh coarsely and place in a serving bowl. Add the tomato, parsley, mint and spring onion and drizzle over the dressing. Gently toss to combine.

Serve with your favourite meat or as mezza with Lebanese bread.

Serves 4

2 medium eggplants

2 medium tomatoes, chopped

½ cup coarsely chopped flat-leaf parsley

¼ cup coarsely chopped mint

2 spring onions, chopped

DRESSING

2 cloves garlic, crushed

¼ cup olive oil

2 tablespoons lemon juice

½ teaspoon salt, or to taste

Hummus

Hummus bi'tahini

- 2 cups dried chickpeas
- 1 teaspoon bicarbonate of soda
- 2 cloves garlic, crushed
- 1½ teaspoons salt, or to taste
- 1½ cups tahini paste
- 1 cup lemon juice
- ½ cup chopped parsley, or a few mint leaves, or pickled turnip, or pickled cucumber, for garnish
- ½ teaspoon paprika
- ½ cup extra virgin olive oil

Hummus bi'tahini is well known and can be found in most supermarkets, but it does not taste as good as homemade. Once you make it a couple of times, it will become so easy to do. It can be frozen for up to six weeks.

Place the chickpeas and bicarbonate of soda in large saucepan and cover with water. Leave to soak overnight.

The next day, drain the chickpeas and rinse well, then add 5 cups water. Bring to the boil over medium–high heat, then reduce the heat and simmer for about 45 minutes, until the chickpeas are soft, topping up the pan with cold water if necessary. Drain and cool.

Place the chickpeas in a food processer (reserving 1 tablespoon whole chickpeas to garnish). Add the garlic, salt, tahini paste and lemon juice and blend for 2–3 minutes, or until the mixture becomes paste-like, scraping the side of the blender occasionally. If the mixture is too hard, add more lemon juice or water.

Spread the paste in a shallow bowl. Decorate with the reserved chickpeas, add the garnish, sprinkle over the paprika and pour the olive oil over the centre.

Serve as a side dish, or with Lebanese bread as part of a mezza.

NOTE: Pickled turnip and cucumber are traditional accompaniments to Lebanese food. They are available at Middle Eastern specialty shops.

Serves 4–6

Baba Ghanouge

Baba ghanouge

Pierce the eggplants with a fork in a few places and place over a direct flame or on top of a gas stove or hot coals to get the smoky taste, turning regularly until blackened. Alternatively, you can bake them in a hot oven at 220°C for 40 minutes, until they become very soft, or microwave on high for 15 minutes.

Separate the skin from the flesh under cold water and discard the skin. Place the flesh in a food processor with the garlic, lemon juice, salt and tahini paste and process for 2 minutes, or until it becomes a paste. Add extra lemon juice if you wish.

Spread the baba ghanouge in a shallow dish, garnish with the parsley and pour the olive oil over the centre.

Serve as a side dish, or with Lebanese bread as part of a mezza.

Serves 4–6

- 3 large eggplants
- 2 cloves garlic, crushed
- ½ cup lemon juice
- 1 teaspoon salt, or to taste
- 1 cup tahini paste
- ¼ cup chopped flat-leaf parsley
- ¼ cup extra virgin olive oil

Garlic Paste

Taratour b'toum

Garlic paste is a must at every Lebanese gathering. Most Lebanese households will have a container of taratour in the fridge.

Place the garlic, salt and potato in food processor and blend on low speed for 2 minutes, until well combined. With the motor running, start adding a bit of oil and a bit of lemon juice, until all the ingredients are combined. You should have a paste-like consistency (see the centre dish on the left).

Stored in a sterilised glass container in the fridge, the paste will keep for 2 weeks, or you can freeze it.

12 cloves garlic, peeled and crushed with a knife

1 teaspoon salt, or to taste

1 small potato, boiled and mashed

1½ cups olive oil

½ cup lemon juice

Yoghurt and Cucumber Dip

Khiyar b'laban

Yoghurt or laban is a major part of the Lebanese diet. I make laban and as soon as one pot finishes I make another. It is always in my fridge and we can use it in soup, have it fresh as a side dish or it can be strained to make labneh (cream cheese).

Coarsely grate the cucumbers and squeeze to drain away any excess liquid. Place the mint, garlic and salt in a mortar and pestle and pound to a fine paste. Transfer to a serving bowl, add the yoghurt and grated cucumber and mix well (see the lower dish on the left).

Serve with your favourite meat.

Makes about 600g

3 Lebanese cucumbers

2 tablespoons finely chopped mint

3 cloves garlic, crushed

½ teaspoon salt, or to taste

500g plain yoghurt

Gnocchi Lebanese Style

Maakroon b'toum

300g plain flour

1 teaspoon salt, or to taste

SAUCE

4 cloves garlic, peeled

1 teaspoon salt, or to taste

½ cup extra virgin olive oil

¼ cup lemon juice

As kids when we were peckish my mother would make maakroon b'toum as it is a quick and simple recipe that would be ready in 15 minutes.

For the sauce, place the garlic and salt in a mortar and pestle and pound to combine. Gradually mix in the olive oil and then the lemon juice. Set aside.

Sift the flour into a large bowl and make a well in the centre. Stir the salt into 220ml warm water, add to the flour and mix well. Turn the dough onto a dusted surface and knead until you have a hard consistency. Divide into 3 pieces and roll each piece into a log 2cm in diameter. Cut the logs into small pieces about 3cm long, and press each piece with your finger on a grater, rolling it towards you. Set aside until all pieces are finished.

Bring 2 litres water to the boil. Add the gnocchi and cook for 10 minutes, or until tender. Drain and transfer to a serving dish. Add the garlic sauce and mix well.

Serve immediately.

NOTE: If you wish, you can toss a can of washed and drained red kidney beans or chickpeas thru the gnocchi before serving. See over the page for step by step pictures of making gnocchi.

Serves 4

Meat Pizza

Lahme b'ajin

Make this dish as a side dish or part of a mezza.

For the base, sift the flour into a large bowl, add the olive oil and mix well with your fingertips. Dissolve the yeast and salt in 300ml warm water and add to the flour. Mix well with your hands and then knead to make the dough. Cover with plastic wrap and leave to rest for 2 hours.

Meanwhile, for the topping, in a bowl combine the onion, garlic, mixed spices, black pepper, sumac, chilli powder if using, pine nuts and pomegranate molasses with your hand. Add the lamb, tomato, salt and olive oil, mix together thoroughly and set aside.

Preheat the oven to 180°C and line a baking tray with baking paper.

Divide the dough in half and roll out one half on a dusted surface to about 3mm thick. Cut into 18 small circles about 7cm in diameter. Place a heaped tablespoon of the meat mixture in the centre of each and spread well. Pinch out four corners of the circles to form squares, and place side-by-side on the baking tray. Repeat with the other half of the dough.

Bake for 20–25 minutes, until golden brown.

Serve hot as a mezza, or with yoghurt and your favourite salad.

NOTE: The meat pizza is pictured at the front of the photo.

Makes about 36

500g plain flour

2 tablespoons olive oil

1 x 7g packet dry yeast

½ teaspoon salt

TOPPING

1 cup finely chopped brown onion

3 cloves garlic, crushed

½ teaspoon Lebanese mixed spices (see page 12)

½ teaspoon black pepper

1 teaspoon sumac

¼ teaspoon chilli powder (optional)

¼ cup pine nuts

1 tablespoon pomegranate molasses

350g lamb mince

1 cup chopped tomatoes

1 teaspoon salt, or to taste

1 tablespoon olive oil

Kafta Pizza

Lahme bil kobez

500g lamb, finely minced

1 brown onion, finely chopped

½ cup finely chopped flat-leaf parsley

2 medium tomatoes, finely chopped

1 tablespoon tomato paste

1 teaspoon salt, or to taste

½ teaspoon black pepper

½ teaspoon Lebanese mixed spices (see page 12)

5 pieces Lebanese bread, or pita bread

A very quick and easy meal, one the kids will love to help you make. It's also nice as a weekend breakfast.

Place the lamb in a large bowl. Add the onion, parsley, tomato, tomato paste, salt, black pepper and mixed spices and mix well to combine (use your hands for a better result).

Place 1 piece of the bread on a board. Spread a portion of the mixture over the bread, covering the entire surface. Place under a preheated grill and grill on medium–high for a few minutes, until the kafta is cooked. Repeat with the remaining bread and mixture until finished.

Serve warm with your favourite salad or yoghurt.

Makes 5

Spinach Triangle
fatayer spanech

Place the flour in a bowl, add the olive oil and mix well with your fingertips. Dissolve the yeast and salt in 300ml warm water and add to the flour. Mix well then knead with your hand to form a dough. Cover with plastic wrap and set aside for 2 hours.

For the filling, wash the spinach and drain well. Chop finely and squeeze out any excess liquid. In a large bowl combine the spinach, brown onion, spring onion, tomato, salt, mixed spices, black pepper, chilli flakes if using, sumac, olive oil and lemon juice and mix well with your hand. Transfer to a colander to drain any excess juice then set aside.

Preheat the oven to 180°C and line a baking tray with baking paper.

Divide the dough into 20 pieces and roll out on a dusted surface into circles of about 10–12cm in diameter. Place 1 tablespoon of the filling in the centre of each circle and fold up to make a triangle, pressing the edges together to seal. Place on the baking tray, brush with the vegetable oil and bake for 15 minutes, or until golden brown.

Serve cold or warm as a mezza, or as a side dish.

Makes about 20

500g plain flour

2 tablespoons olive oil

1 x 7g sachet dry yeast

½ teaspoon salt

FILLING

2 bunches English spinach

1 medium brown onion, finely chopped

2 spring onions, finely chopped

1 large tomato, finely chopped

1 teaspoon salt, or to taste

½ teaspoon Lebanese mixed spices (see page 12)

½ teaspoon black pepper

¼ teaspoon dried chilli flakes (optional)

1 teaspoon sumac

2 tablespoons olive oil

1 tablespoon lemon juice

2 tablespoons vegetable oil

Pastry with Lamb

Sambousik

- 500g plain flour
- 2 tablespoons olive oil
- 1 x 7g sachet dry yeast
- ½ teaspoon salt

FILLING

- 25g butter
- ½ cup pine nuts
- 1 brown onion, finely chopped
- 3 cloves garlic, finely chopped
- 300g lamb mince
- 1 teaspoon salt, or to taste
- ½ teaspoon Lebanese mixed spices (see page 12)
- ½ teaspoon white pepper
- 1 tablespoon pomegranate molasses
- vegetable oil, for deep frying

Place the flour in a bowl, add the olive oil and mix well with your fingertips. Dissolve the yeast and salt in 300ml warm water and add to the flour. Mix well then knead with your hand to form a dough. Cover with plastic wrap and set aside for 2 hours.

Meanwhile, for the filling, melt the butter in a frying pan. Add the pine nuts and cook until light golden. Add the onion and garlic and cook for 2 minutes, then add the lamb and the salt and cook for 20 minutes, stirring occasionally. Add the mixed spices and white pepper and remove from the heat. Stir in the pomegranate molasses and mix well, then transfer to a colander to drain any excess liquid. Set aside.

Roll out the dough until very thin, about 4mm thick. Cut in 6cm diameter circles and place 1 tablespoon of the filling in each circle. Fold the circles in half, using a fork to press the two sides together or your index finger to fold the edge inwards, making sure they are sealed well. Continue until all the meat and dough is used.

Fry in batches in a deep-fryer on medium heat until lightly golden brown.

Serve as an appetiser or mezza.

NOTE: *Sambousik* can be frozen for up to 3 months.

Makes about 65

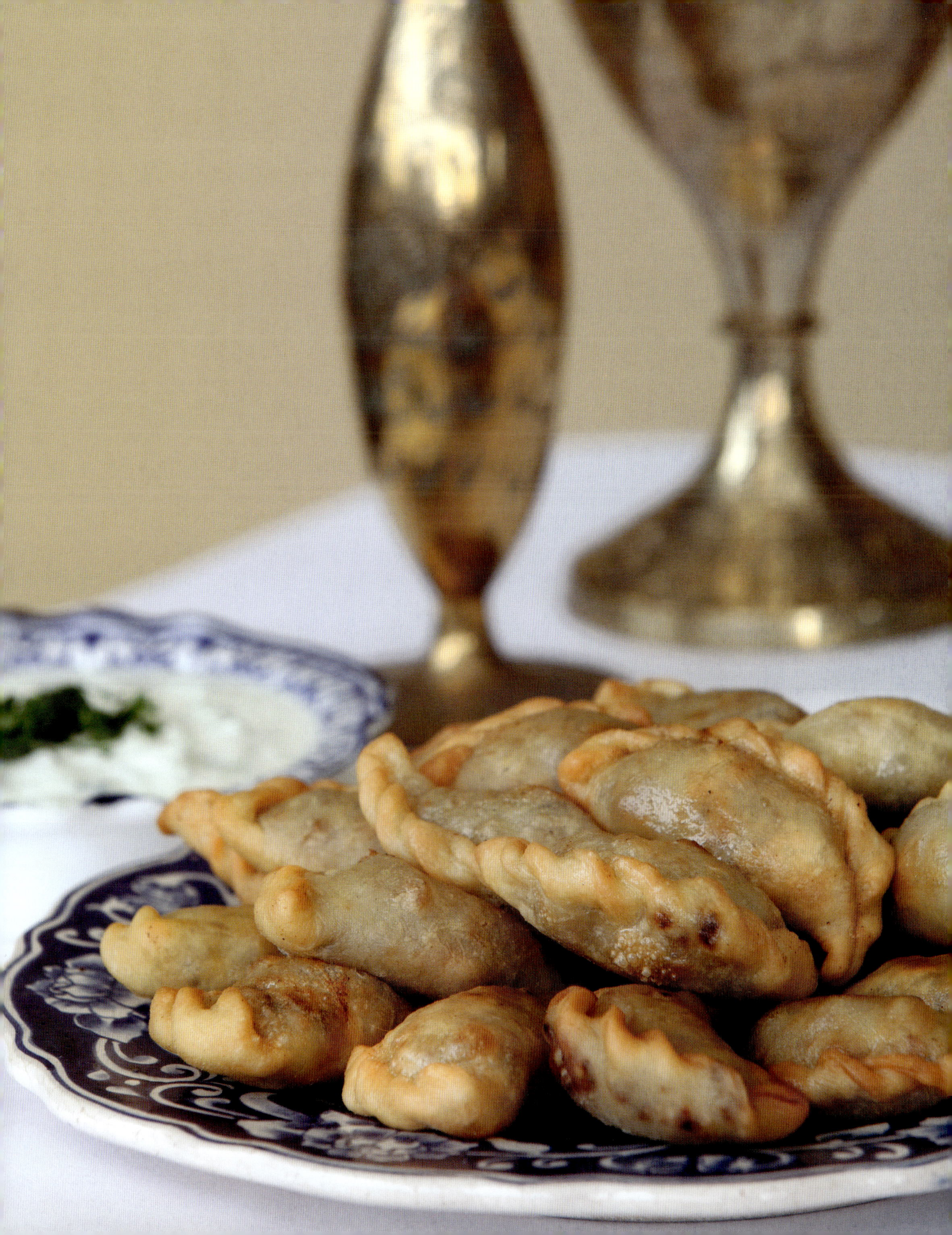

Zaater Pizza

Manaheesh b'zaater

500g plain flour

2 tablespoons olive oil

1 x 7g sachet dry yeast

½ teaspoon salt

TOPPING

½ cup dry zaater (available at Lebanese shops)

½ cup olive oil

When I was growing up manaheesh b'zaater was my favourite breakfast with hot sweet tea. Zaater is made from thyme, oregano, sumac and sesame seeds. Thyme and oregano grow wild in the mountains in Lebanon. Everyone collects their own and then dries them, pounds them in the jirin with a moddaqqa (mortar and pestle) until very fine then adds salt, sumac and roasted sesame seeds. Zaater can keep for 12 months in an air-tight jar.

Place the flour in a bowl, add the olive oil and mix well with your fingertips. Dissolve the yeast and salt in 300ml warm water and add to the flour. Mix well then knead with your hand to form a dough. Cover with plastic wrap and set aside for 2 hours.

For the topping, mix the zaater with the olive oil and set aside.

Preheat the oven to 220°C and line a baking tray with baking paper.

Divide the dough into 10 pieces and roll out into circles about 9cm in diameter. Cover and set aside to rest for 10 minutes.

Spoon 1 tablespoon of the topping over each pastry circle, then use your fingers to spread the mixture and gently press into the pastry. Place on the baking tray and bake for 10 minutes, or until golden.

Serve as they are or spread with thick yoghurt, or if you wish, add chopped tomato and crumbled feta cheese.

Makes 10

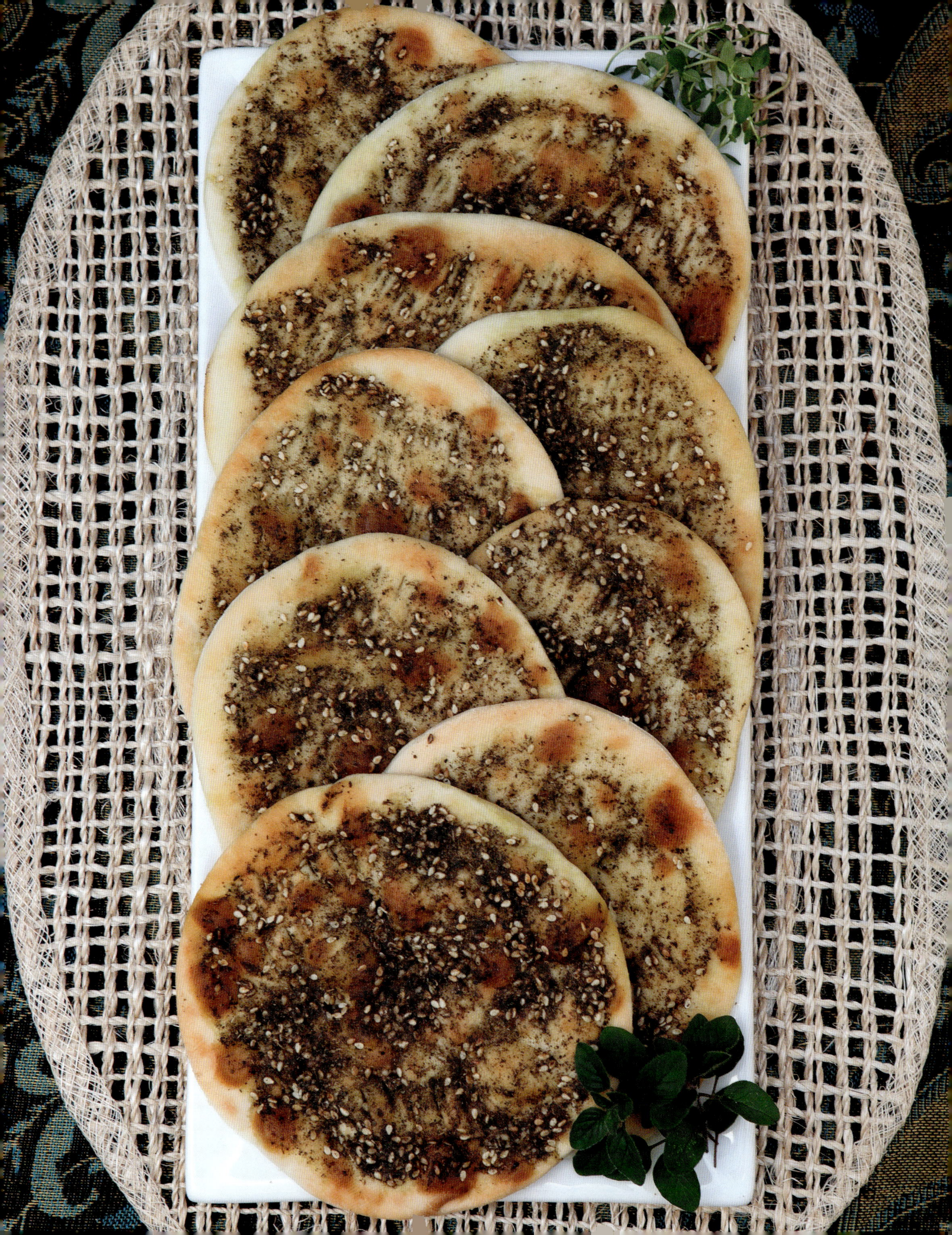

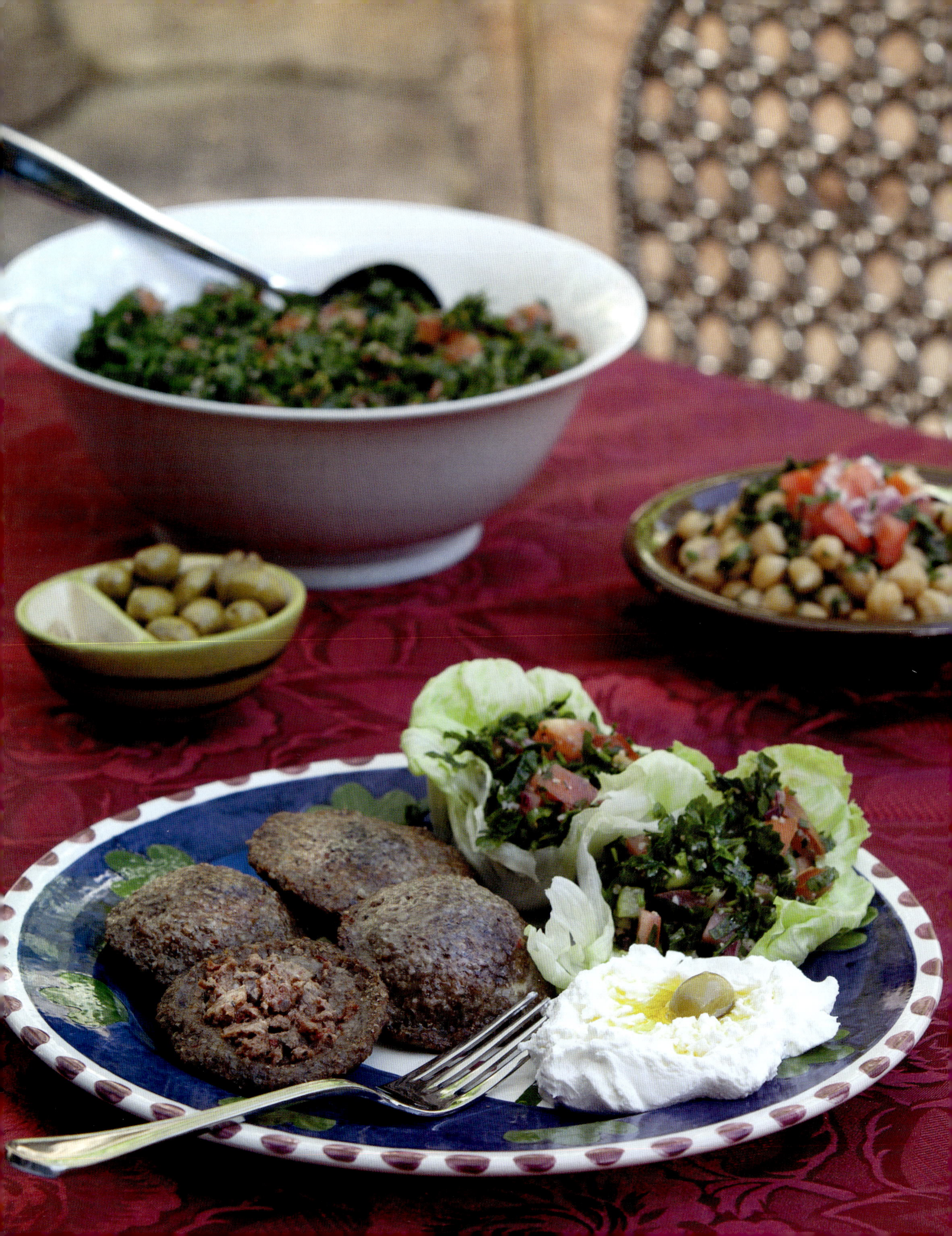

Kibbee (plain)
Kibbeh

Kibbee is Lebanon's national dish. We used to have kibbee at least once a week, made in different ways. Of all the kibbee dishes, kibbeh ou'ras is my favourite!

Wash and drain the burghul and squeeze out any excess water.

Place the onion, mint, capsicum, chilli if using, salt and all the spices in a food processor. Process at high speed until very fine, then add the lamb and process to a paste. Add the burghul and mix well for 2–3 minutes.

Transfer to a bowl and knead the mixture until it is well combined, wetting your fingers occasionally to prevent the mixture sticking to your hand.

NOTE: Kibbee mixed spices are available at Lebanese specialty shops. This is the base recipe for the following kibbee dishes.

2 cups burghul (crushed wheat)

1 medium brown onion, chopped

¼ cup chopped mint

½ red capsicum, chopped

1 red chilli (optional)

1 tablespoon salt, or to taste

1 teaspoon kibbee mixed spices

½ teaspoon black pepper

¼ teaspoon ground cumin

¼ teaspoon Lebanese mixed spices (see page 12)

500g ground lean lamb, all sinew removed (available from Lebanese butchers)

Grilled Kibbee
Kibbeh ou'ras

For the filling, place all the ingredients in a food processor and blend for 3 minutes, until well combined. Set aside.

Make 2 small patties from the kibbee mixture, about 10cm in diameter and 8mm thick. Place 1 tablespoon of the filling on 1 patty and then cover with the second patty and seal well. Repeat until all the mixture is used. Cook under a hot grill or barbecue over charcoal.

Serve with tabbouli salad (see page 11) or yoghurt.

Makes 12–14

1 quantity plain kibbee (see above)

FILLING

250g lamb fat, minced

1 medium brown onion, grated

¼ cup chopped mint

½ red capsicum, chopped

½ teaspoon salt, or to taste

¼ teaspoon Lebanese mixed spices (see page 12)

¼ teaspoon black pepper

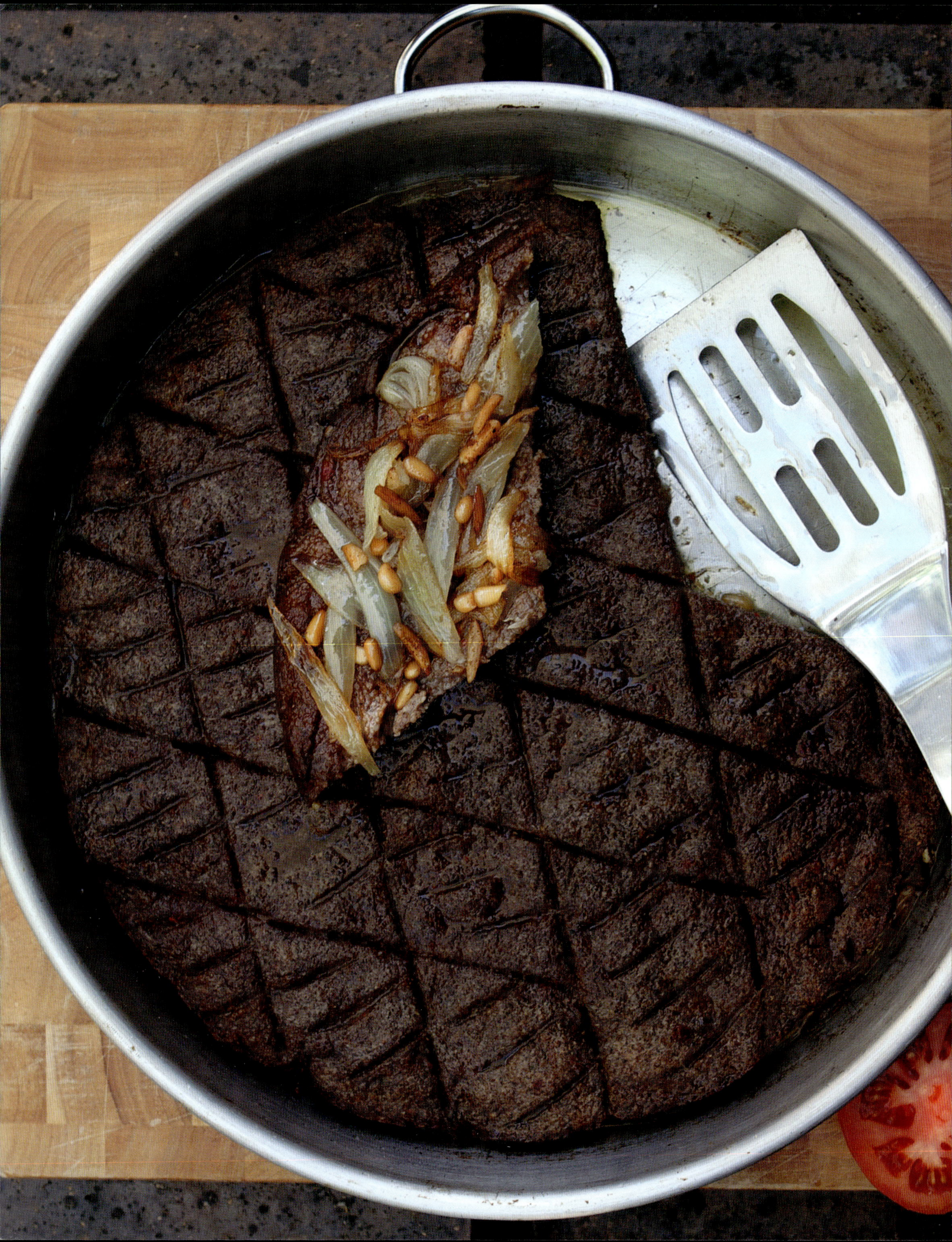

Baked Kibbee with Onion and Pine Nuts
Kibbeh b' sayneyeh

Preheat the oven to 200°C and generously grease a 30cm round baking dish with olive oil, making sure the side is well oiled.

Heat ¼ cup olive oil in a frying pan over low heat. Add the pine nuts and cook until golden brown, stirring constantly to prevent them burning. Remove from the pan and set aside. Add the onion to the pan and cook for about 4 minutes, or until light brown. Remove the pan from the heat, add the pine nuts, black pepper and mixed spices and combine well. Transfer to the prepared baking dish and spread evenly to cover the base.

For the kibbee, use your hands to make small patties about 1cm thick, and place them close together over the onion base, making sure all the onion is covered. Smooth out the surface, wetting your hand to prevent the kibbee sticking to your fingers. Mark the top with parallel cuts on the diagonal about 6cm apart, then cut on the diagonal the other way to create diamond shapes. Pour the vegetable oil over the top and use the tip of a round-edge knife to mark a small dent in the middle of each diamond.

Bake for 30–40 minutes, until golden brown.

Serve hot or cold, with salad or yoghurt.

Serves 4–6

¼ cup olive oil

½ cup pine nuts

2 medium brown onions, finely sliced

¼ teaspoon black pepper

¼ teaspoon Lebanese mixed spices (see page 12)

¾ cup vegetable oil

1 quantity plain kibbee (see page 41)

Kibbee Balls
Kibbeh kebakib

2 tablespoons butter

½ cup pine nuts

1 large brown onion, finely chopped

300g lamb mince

1 teaspoon salt, or to taste

½ teaspoon Lebanese mixed spices (see page 12)

½ teaspoon black pepper

1 quantity plain kibbee (see page 41)

2 cups vegetable oil, for deep-frying

Place 1 tablespoon of the butter in a frying pan, add the pine nuts and cook for a few minutes over low heat, until golden brown, stirring constantly to avoid burning. Remove with a slotted spoon and place on paper towel to drain. Using the same pan, add the remaining butter and the onion and cook for 3–4 minutes, until the onion is translucent. Add the lamb and cook for 20–25 minutes, stirring occasionally. Add the pine nuts, salt, mixed spices and black pepper. Mix well and remove from the heat.

To make the *kebakib*, divide the kibbee mixture into small, walnut-sized balls. Place one ball in the palm of your hand, dip your index finger in cold water and insert it into the centre of the ball, turning constantly to make a hollow. Place 1 teaspoonful of the lamb filling in the hollow and close the end to form an egg shape, smoothing the surface well to prevent any filling escaping. Repeat until all the kibbee mixture is used.

Cook in the vegetable oil in a deep-fryer or deep-sided frying pan for about 5 minutes, or until golden brown.

Serve with a green salad or yoghurt and cucumber dip or as part of a mezza.

NOTE: The *kebakib* will keep in the freezer for 6 weeks.

Makes about 30

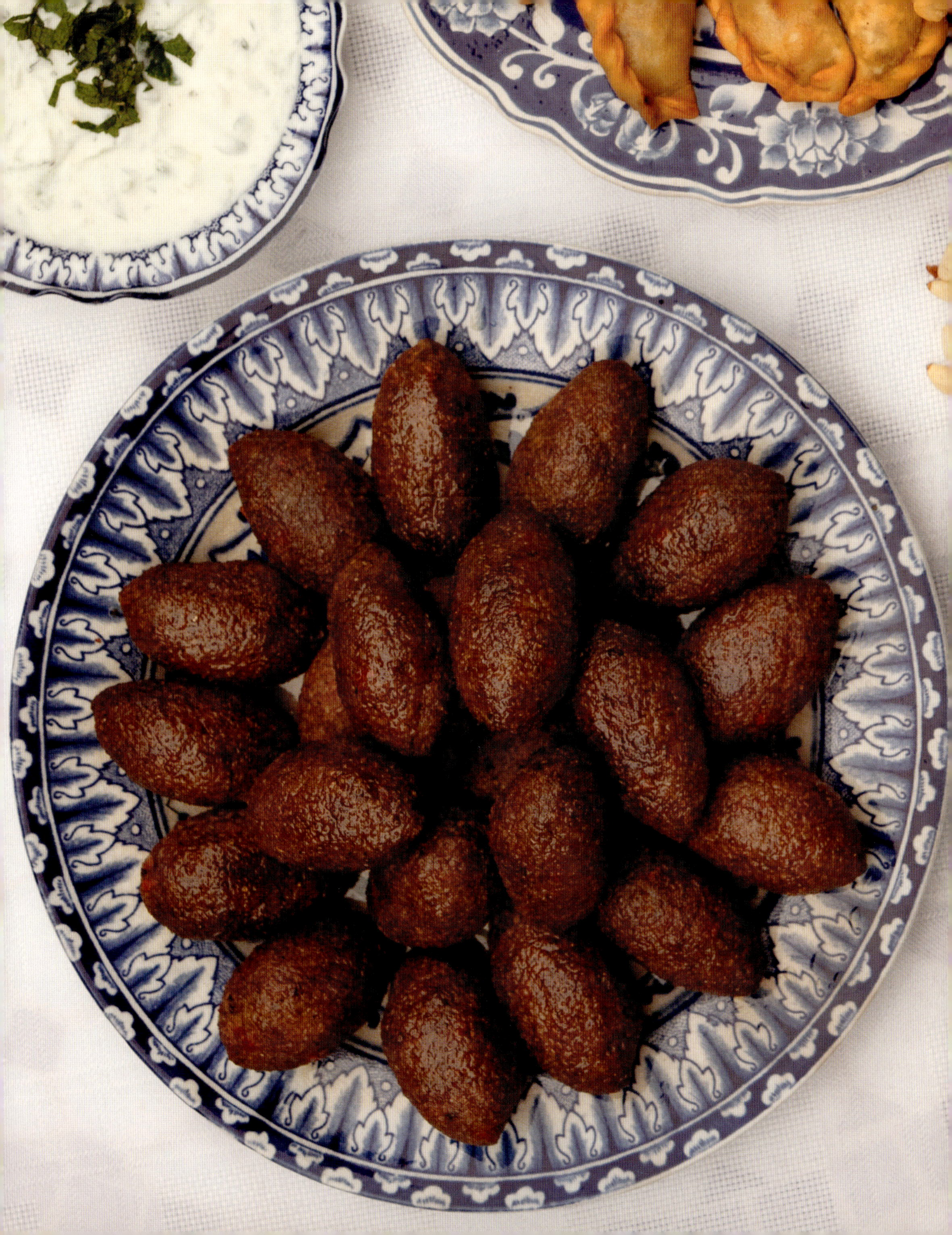

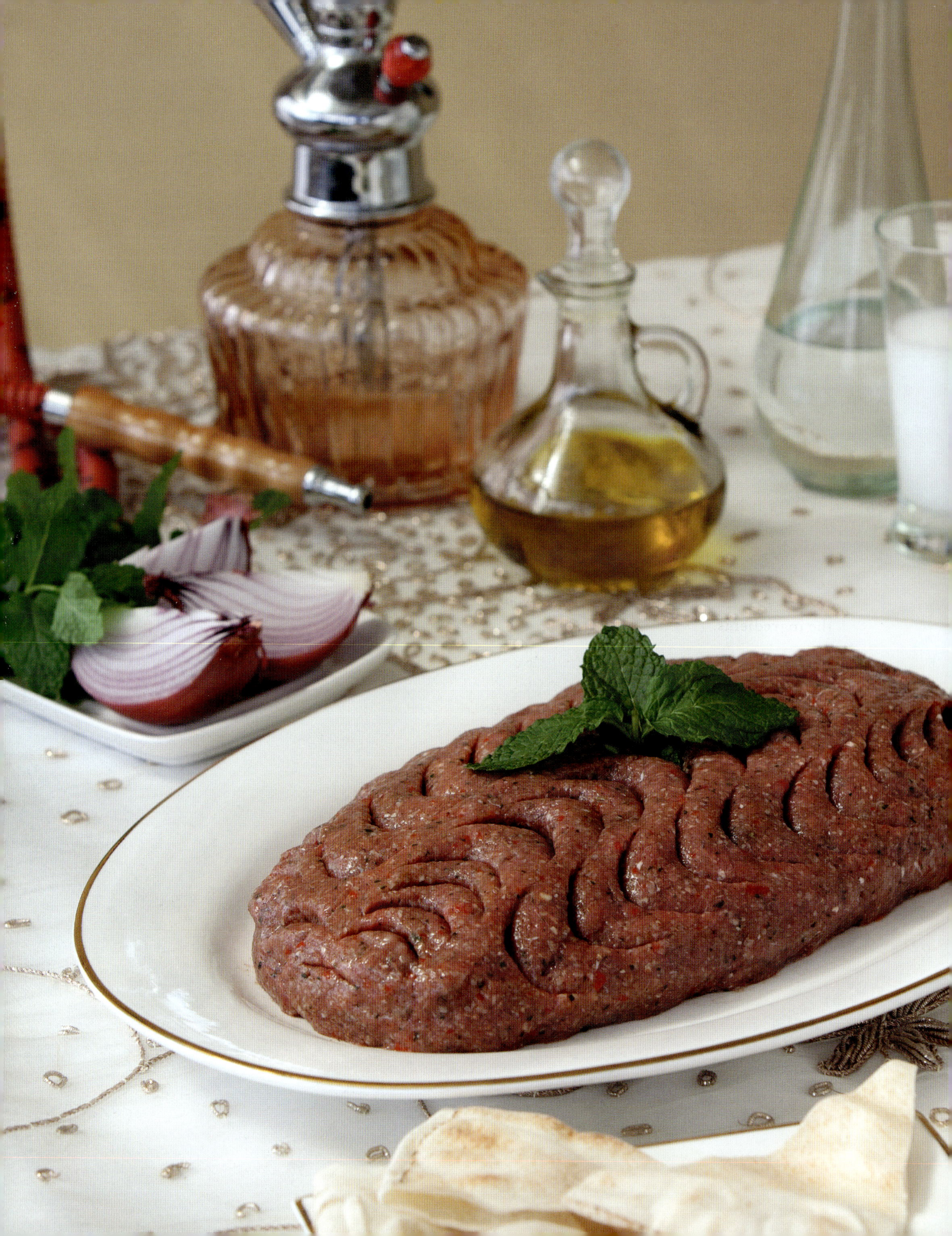

Kibbee Raw
Kibbeh nayye

When my mother made this she would use the big jirin and moddaqqa, a stone mortar 50cm high by 40cm wide and the wooden moddaqqa, and you could hear her pounding it blocks away. The neighbours would come to our house and say, 'Is the kibbee ready?' In Lebanon people exchange plates of food — you give them a plate of whatever lunch was on the menu and they would return the plate, full of food they had cooked or baked that day.

Wash and drain the burghul, and squeeze out any excess water.

Place the brown onion, chopped mint, capsicum, chilli if using, salt, black pepper and mixed spices in a food processor and process at high speed for 2 minutes. Add the lamb and process again until you have a paste. Add the burghul and process for another minute, adding half the chilled water to help combine the ingredients.

Transfer to a bowl and knead well, wetting your hand with chilled water to prevent the mixture sticking to your fingers. Place the mixture on a serving plate and shape it into a round or oval depending on the shape of the plate. Use a fork to decorate with a design and garnish with the whole mint leaves.

Serve with extra virgin olive oil, sliced red onion and Lebanese bread.

Serves 6–8

1 cup burghul (crushed wheat)

1 medium brown onion, chopped

¼ cup chopped mint, plus extra whole leaves, for garnish

½ red capsicum, chopped

1 small red chilli, chopped (optional)

1½ teaspoons salt, or to taste

½ teaspoon ground black pepper

½ teaspoon kibbee mixed spices (available at Lebanese shops)

800g very lean lamb fillets, fat trimmed, cut into cubes

½ cup chilled water

1 cup extra virgin olive oil

1 red onion, sliced

Lebanese bread

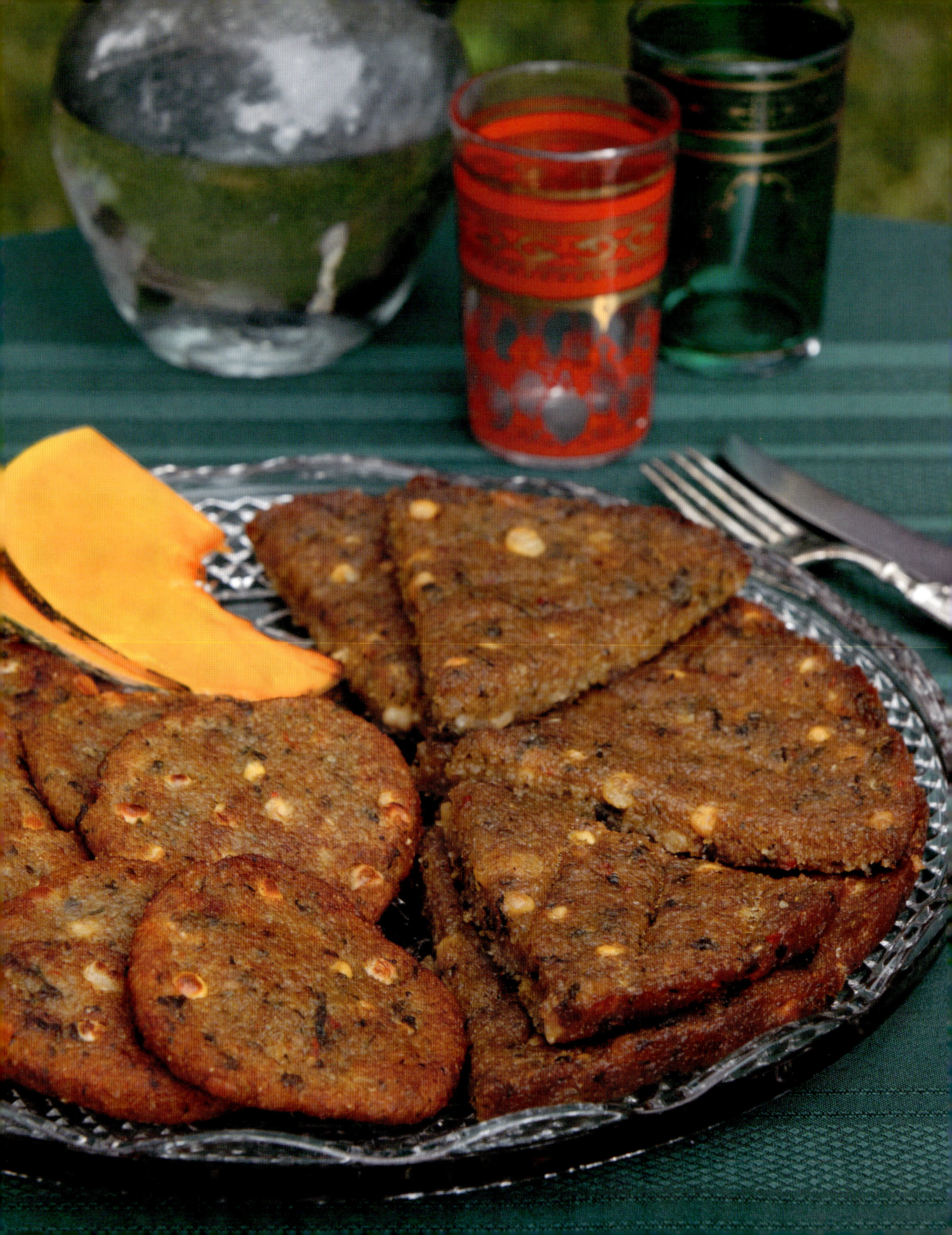

Kibbee Pumpkin (vegetarian)
Kibbeh heeleh

This dish is part of the menu on Good Friday.

Preheat the oven to 200°C and grease a 30cm baking tray with the olive oil, including the sides.

Chop up the pumpkin and potatoes and boil over medium heat until tender. Drain well.

Place the onion, mint, parsley and coriander in a food processor and process for 1 minute. Add the salt and all the spices with the pumpkin and potato and process for 2 minutes. Add the burghul and mix well to combine.

Transfer to a bowl, add the flour and the chickpeas and mix until well combined, wetting your hand with cold water to prevent the mixture sticking to your fingers.

Pour the mixture into the baking tray and smooth the surface. Cut into 8 slices and add the oil. Bake for 30–40 minutes, until golden brown.

Serve warm or cold, with green salad or a yoghurt salad.

NOTE: You can also shape the mixture into patties, about 8cm in diameter, and fry in hot oil on both sides until golden brown.

Serves 6

2 tablespoons olive oil

400g pumpkin

300g potatoes

1 medium brown onion, chopped

¼ cup chopped mint

½ cup chopped flat-leaf parsley

¼ cup chopped coriander

2 teaspoons salt, or to taste

½ teaspoon Lebanese mixed spices (see page 12)

½ teaspoon black pepper

½ teaspoon ground cumin

1½ cups burghul (crushed wheat), washed and drained

1½ cups plain flour

½ cup dried split chickpeas, soaked in water overnight, washed and drained

¾ cup vegetable oil, for baking or frying

Kibbee Fish

Kibbet el'samak

1 teaspoon salt, or to taste

½ bunch coriander, finely chopped

2 teaspoons chopped mint

1 medium brown onion, finely chopped

2 tablespoons finely chopped red capsicum

1 small chilli, chopped (optional)

500g boneless fish fillets (such as John Dory or barramundi), cut into 3cm chunks

1 cup burghul (crushed wheat), washed and drained

grated zest of 1 lemon

½ teaspoon ground cumin

½ teaspoon Lebanese mixed spices (see page 12)

½ teaspoon black pepper

½ cup olive oil, for baking

FILLING

¼ cup olive oil

½ cup pine nuts

2 medium brown onions, sliced lengthways

¼ teaspoon Lebanese mixed spices

½ teaspoon ground cumin

For the filling, heat the olive oil in a frying pan. Add the pine nuts and cook over low heat until they start to change colour. Remove with a slotted spoon. Add the onion to the pan and cook for a few minutes until very lightly browned. Remove the pan from the heat, add the pine nuts and spices and mix well. Set aside.

Preheat the oven to 200°C and generously grease a 30cm baking tray with olive oil, including the sides.

Place the salt, coriander, mint, onion, capsicum and chilli if using in a food processor and process for 1 minute. Add the fish and process to a paste. Add the burghul, lemon zest and all the spices and process for a further minute. Transfer to a bowl and mix until well combined, wetting your hand with cold water to prevent the mixture sticking to your fingers.

Spread the filling evenly over the base of the baking tray. Make small patties, about 1cm thick, of the fish mixture and place side-by-side over the top, leaving no gaps between the patties, and smooth out the surface. (See Baked Kibbee with Onion and Pine Nuts, on page 43, for photographs of this step.) Cut into 8 triangular slices or shallow diamond shapes 6cm wide x 6cm long. Drizzle over the olive oil and bake for 40 minutes, or until golden brown.

To serve, turn the slices upside down onto a serving platter and accompany with a garden salad.

Serves 6–8

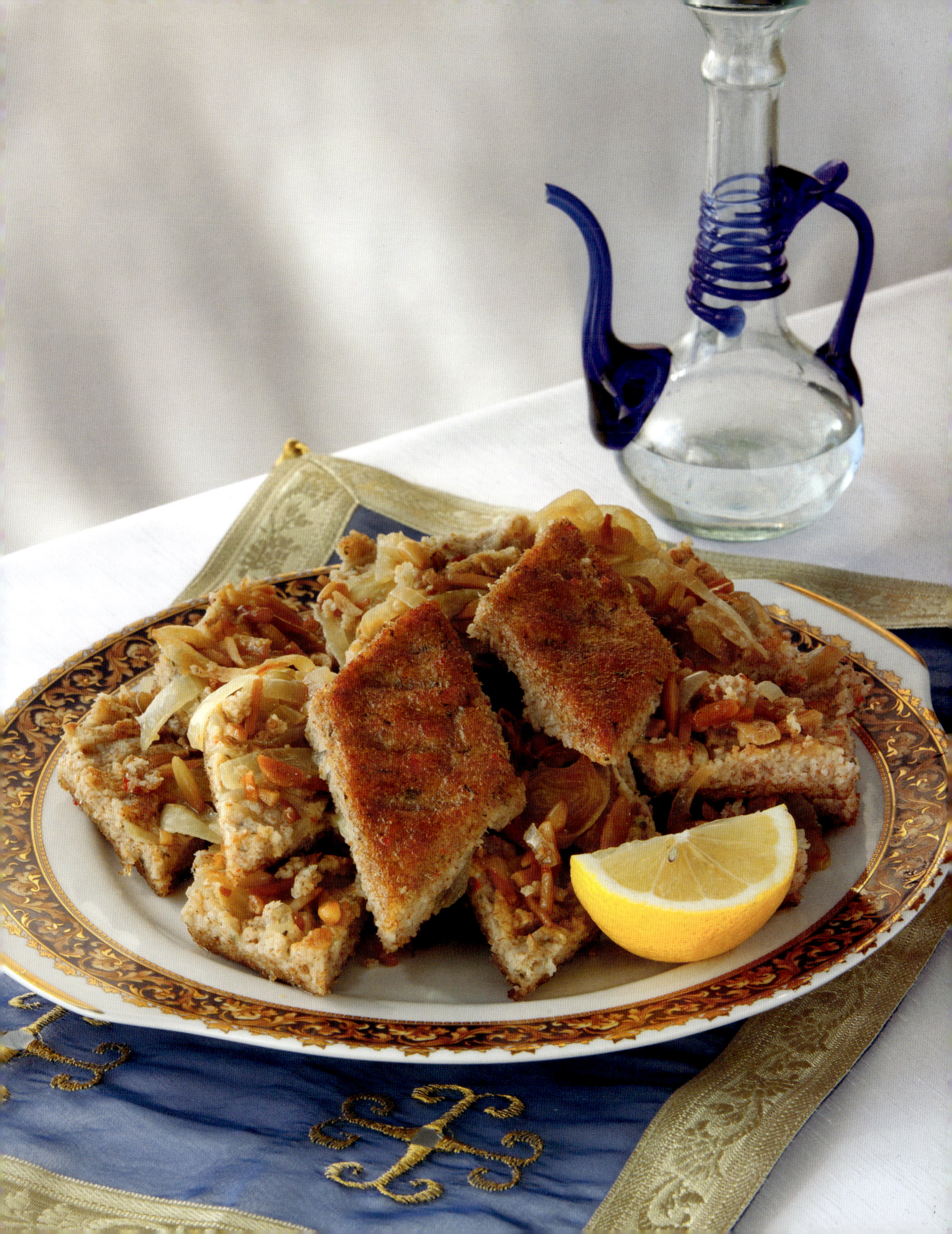

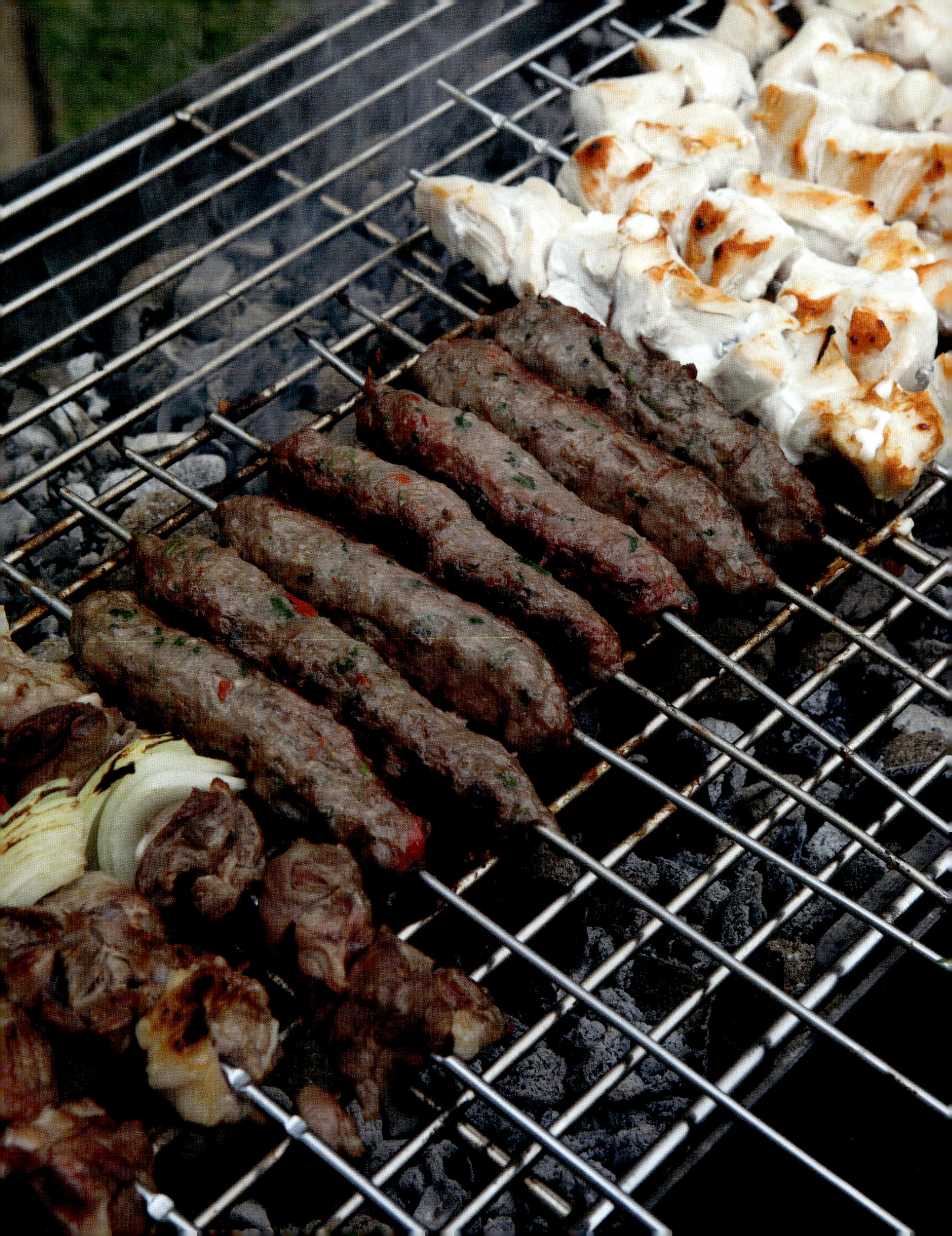

Kafta Kebab

Kafta meshwy

Kafta is always present at every barbecue. The kids and the adults love it equally.

Combine all the ingredients in a bowl, wetting your hand with cold water to prevent the mixture sticking to your fingers. Roll the mixture into a thick sausage shape and thread onto wooden or metal skewers. Barbecue or chargrill over high heat for a few minutes on each side, until cooked.

Serve immediately with tabbouli salad (see page 11), green salad and hummus (see page 20) on Lebanese bread. Or open the bread, spread with the hummus dip, place the kafta on top, add 2 tablespoons each of tabbouli and garden salad, then roll the bread to make a wrap and enjoy.

Makes 16–18

1kg lean lamb, finely minced

1 medium brown onion, grated

2 cups finely chopped flat-leaf parsley (about 1 bunch)

1 tablespoon salt, or to taste

½ teaspoon black pepper

1 teaspoon Lebanese mixed spices (see page 12)

1 tablespoon sumac

Kafta with Eggs
Kafta baayd

- 1kg lean lamb, minced or ground in food processor
- 1 teaspoon salt, or to taste
- 1 teaspoon black pepper
- ½ teaspoon Lebanese mixed spices (see page 12)
- 4 hard-boiled eggs, shelled
- 2 tablespoons olive oil, for frying
- 400g can diced tomatoes

Thoroughly combine the lamb, salt, black pepper and mixed spices in a bowl. Divide the mixture into 4 balls then flatten out 1 ball until it is large enough to cover an egg, wetting your hand and the work surface so the mixture doesn't stick. Place 1 egg in the centre and roll the meat over to completely cover it. Repeat the process with the remaining 3 eggs and mixture.

Heat the olive oil in a non-stick deep-sided frying pan over medium–high heat. Add the kafta and cook on all sides to seal the meat. Add the diced tomato and 1 cup water, season to taste with salt and black pepper, reduce the heat and simmer on low for 45 minutes, or until the meat is cooked.

Serve with mashed potato and your favourite vegetables.

NOTE: You can substitute the eggs with 1 cup chopped flat-leaf parsley and 8 cloves garlic, sliced.

Makes 4

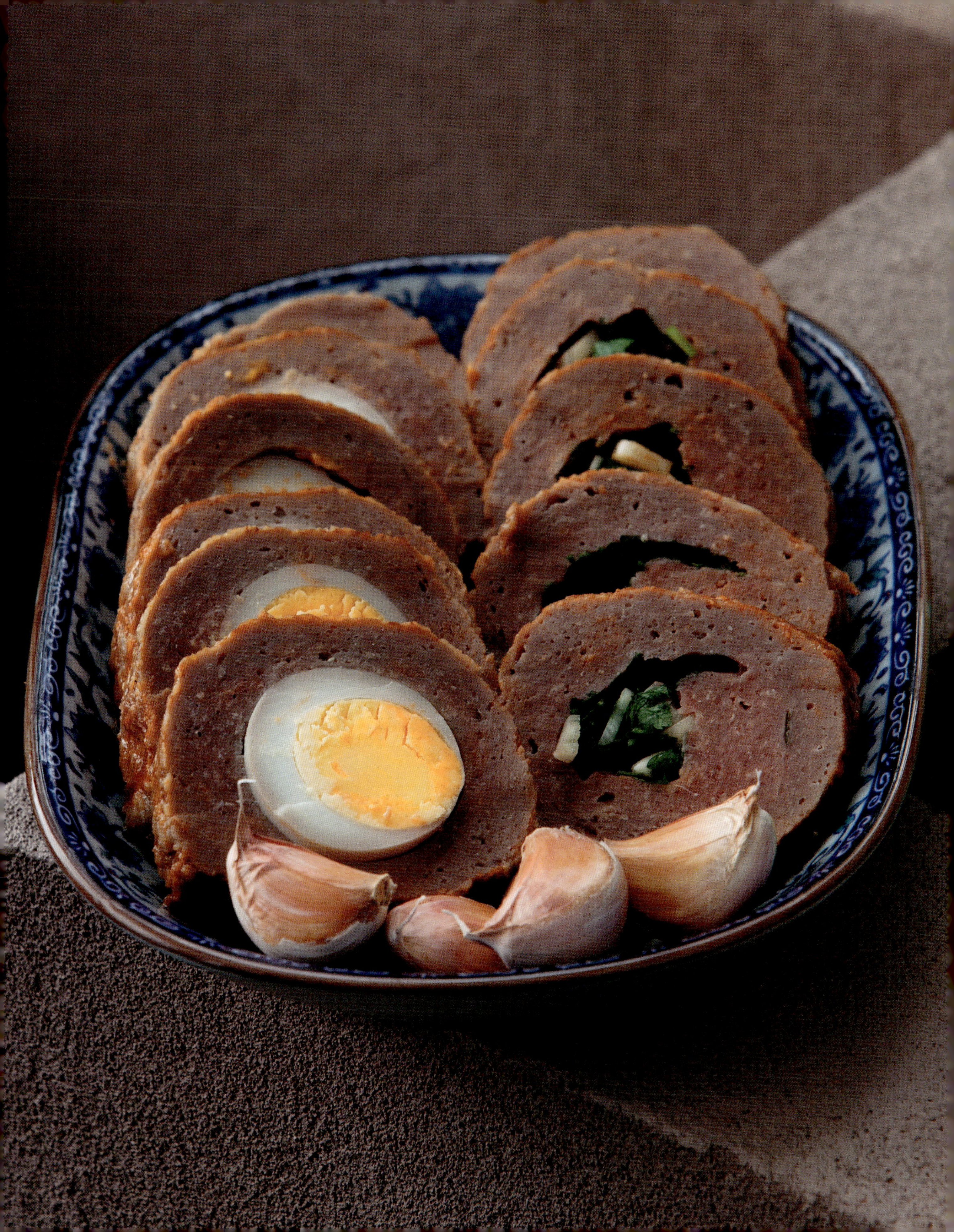

Lamb Kebab

Lahme meshwy

1kg lean lamb, cut into 3cm cubes

1 teaspoon salt, or to taste

1 teaspoon black pepper

2 tablespoons olive oil

2 tablespoons dried oregano

4 small brown onions, quartered

1 red capsicum, cut into 3cm squares (optional)

1 green capsicum, cut into 3cm squares (optional)

GARNISH (OPTIONAL)

2 medium brown onions, sliced

½ cup chopped flat-leaf parsley

2 teaspoons sumac

For the garnish, mix the onion, parsley and sumac together with your fingers to bruise the onion. Set aside.

Place the lamb in a bowl, add the salt, black pepper, olive oil and oregano. Mix together well and leave to marinate for a minimum of 2 hours.

Thread the lamb and vegetables onto metal or bamboo skewers, in the order of two meat cubes then one vegetable, until all the ingredients are used. Chargrill or barbecue over high heat for a few minutes on each side until cooked.

Serve warm with tabbouli salad (see page 11), or green salad on Lebanese bread, or with the garnish.

NOTE: See over the page for picture.

Makes 12

Garlic Chicken
Shish tawook

Place the garlic and salt in a mortar and pestle and pound until smooth. Add the olive oil and lemon juice and mix well.

Place the chicken in a large bowl, add the garlic paste and leave to marinate for a minimum of 2 hours.

Thread the chicken onto bamboo or metal skewers and barbecue or chargrill over high heat for a few minutes on each side.

Serve warm with a garden salad or tabbouli salad (see page 11) on Lebanese bread.

NOTE: See over the page for picture.

Serves 4–6

5 cloves garlic, crushed

1 tablespoon salt, or to taste

¼ cup olive oil

¼ cup lemon juice

1kg chicken breast fillets, cut into 3cm cubes

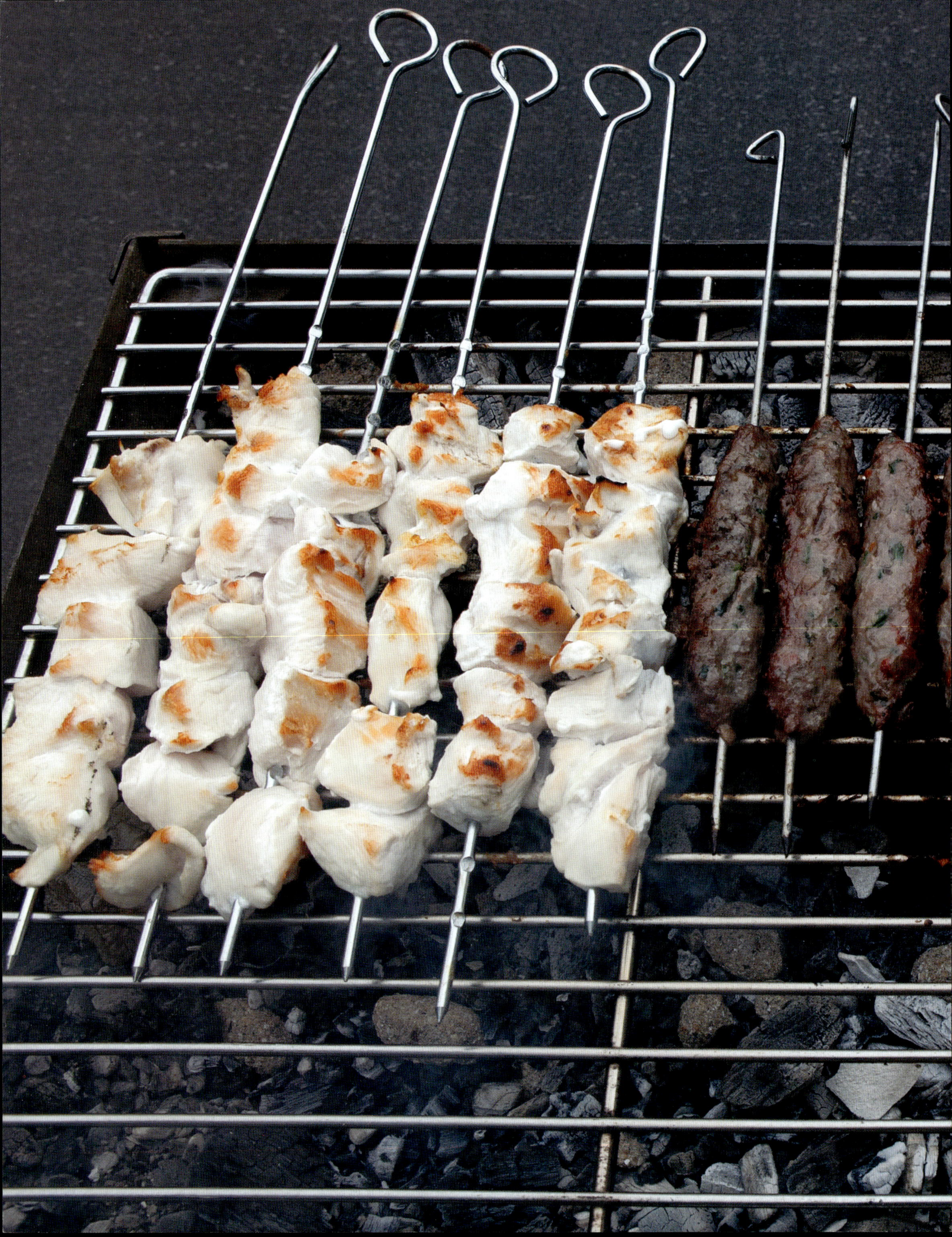

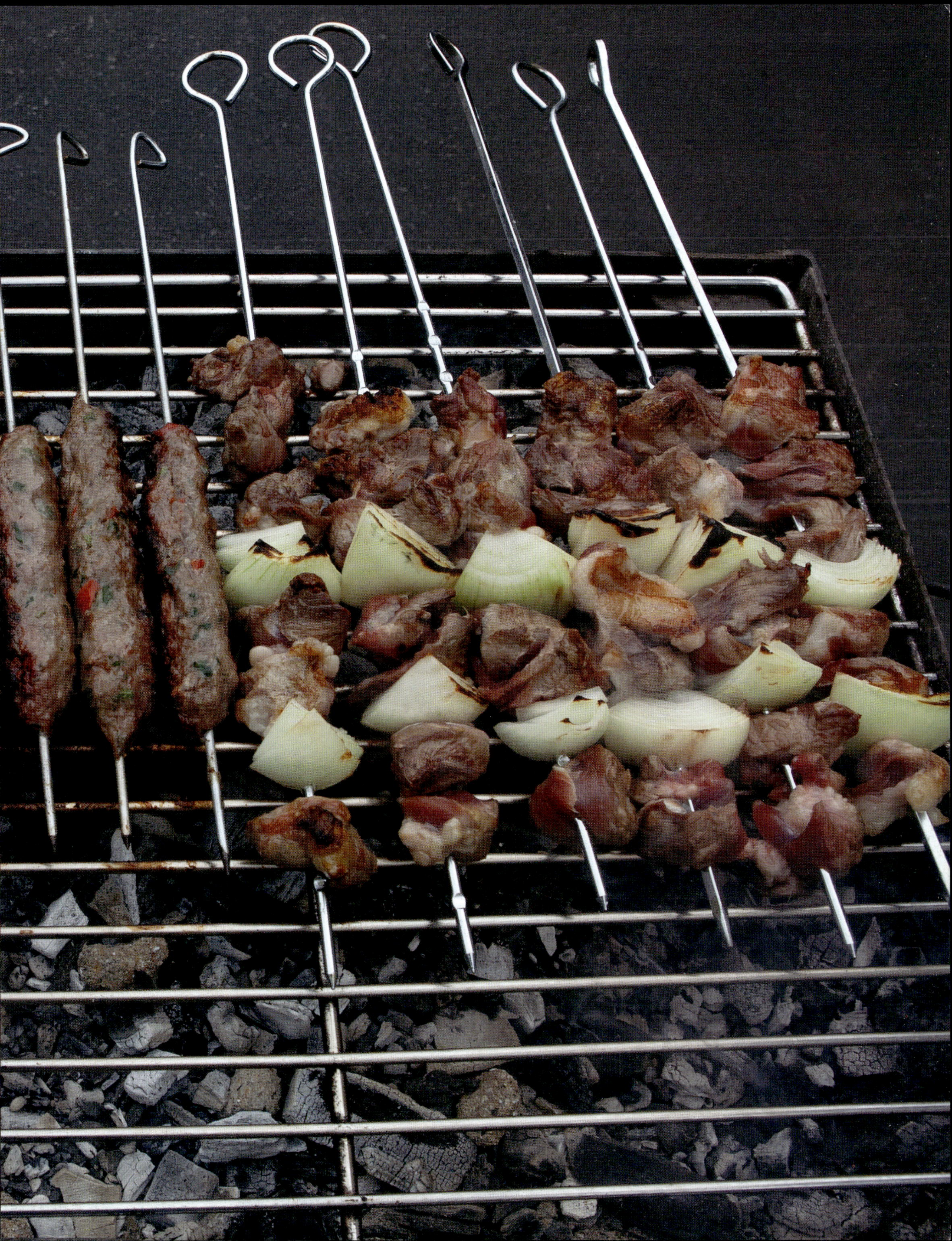

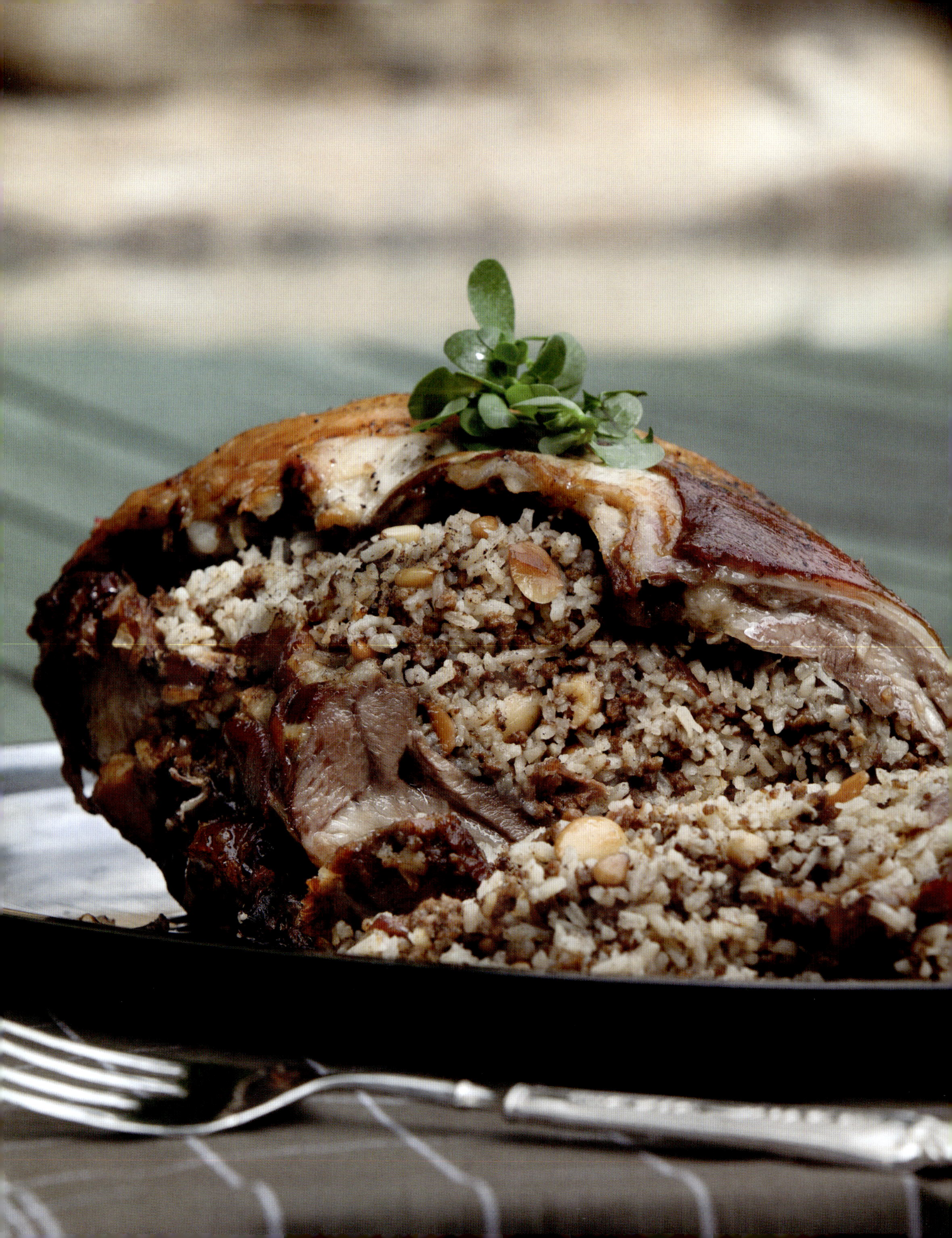

Stuffed Rib and Lamb Shoulder
Dela'ah mehshi

Heat the butter in a saucepan over medium heat. Add the almonds and pine nuts and sauté until lightly browned. Remove with a slotted spoon and set aside. Add 1 tablespoon of the olive oil and the onion to the pan and cook until translucent. Add the lamb mince and cook for 10 minutes, then add the rice, 1 teaspoon salt, ½ teaspoon black pepper and the mixed spices and cook for a few more minutes. Add the pine nuts and almonds and 2 cups water. Bring to the boil then reduce the heat and simmer for about 10 minutes, until all the water has evaporated.

Preheat the oven to 200°C and line a baking dish with baking paper.

Remove any excess fat from the shoulder and ribs and spread on a flat board. Fold the ribs over the shoulder and use a strong needle and thread to sew up the side to make a pocket. Place the rice stuffing in the pocket and then continue sewing up the side to prevent the rice escaping. Season with the remaining olive oil, salt and black pepper.

Wrap the lamb in aluminium foil and place in the baking dish. Add 2 cups water to the tray and bake for 1 hour. Reduce the oven temperature to 160°C and add another cup of water. Bake for 2½ hours, adding a cup of water every half hour to keep the lamb moist.

Remove from the pan and set aside to rest for 10 minutes before uncovering and cutting into thick slices.

Serve warm with cooked vegetables or your favourite salad.

Serves 8–10

30g butter

¼ cup almonds, halved

¼ cup pine nuts

2 tablespoons olive oil

1 medium brown onion, finely chopped

250g coarse lamb mince

1½ cups long grain rice, rinsed and drained

1½ teaspoons salt, or to taste

1 teaspoon black pepper

¼ teaspoon Lebanese mixed spices (see page 12)

3.5kg boneless lamb shoulder and ribs, in one piece

Pearl Couscous with Lamb and Chicken

Moghrabieh

- 500g leg lamb chops (about 4 chops), trimmed and cut in half
- 1 teaspoon salt, or to taste
- 2 cinnamon sticks
- 40g butter
- 10 pickling onions, peeled
- 2 cups pearl couscous (*moghrabieh*), soaked overnight in 4 cups chicken stock
- ½ cup chickpeas, soaked and then boiled until tender, or 400g can chickpeas, rinsed and drained
- ½ teaspoon black pepper
- 1 teaspoon Lebanese mixed spices (see page 12)
- 1 teaspoon ground cumin
- 1 teaspoon ground caraway
- 1 teaspoon ground cinnamon

We use a lot of spices in this dish. Moghrabieh can be made with chicken or lamb, or both.

Place the lamb in 5 cups water with the salt and cinnamon sticks and bring to the boil, then reduce the heat and simmer for 1 hour, removing any scum from the surface, until tender.

Heat half the butter in a large saucepan until it changes colour, add the onions and cook for a few minutes then remove and add to the stock in the meat pan. Cook them for 10 minutes then remove with a slotted spoon and keep warm.

Heat the remaining butter, add the drained couscous and cook for 10 minutes, stirring constantly. Add the chickpeas and onions and cook for a further 5 minutes. Add 1 cup of the stock from the lamb, stirring constantly to prevent the mixture sticking to the pan. Add the black pepper, mixed spices, cumin and caraway, stir well to combine and remove from the heat.

Transfer the *moghrabieh* to a large serving dish, arrange the lamb and onions on top and garnish with the ground cinnamon. Serve with a jug of extra meat stock if you wish.

NOTE: You can also fry 250g chicken breast fillet strips (about 6cm x 3cm) in 2 tablespoons butter for about 3 minutes on each side and arrange them on top of the moghrabieh with the lamb and onions.

Serves 4–6

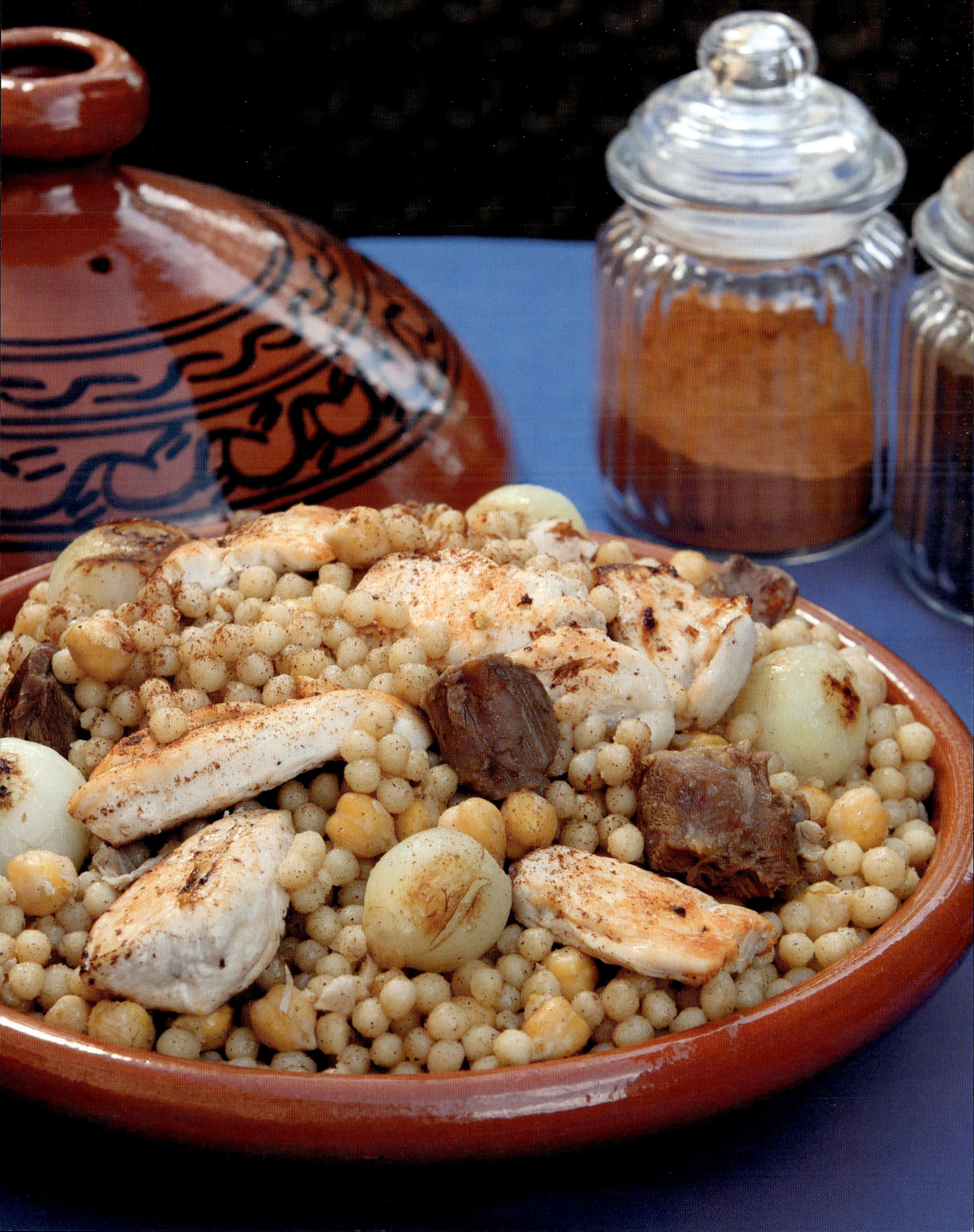

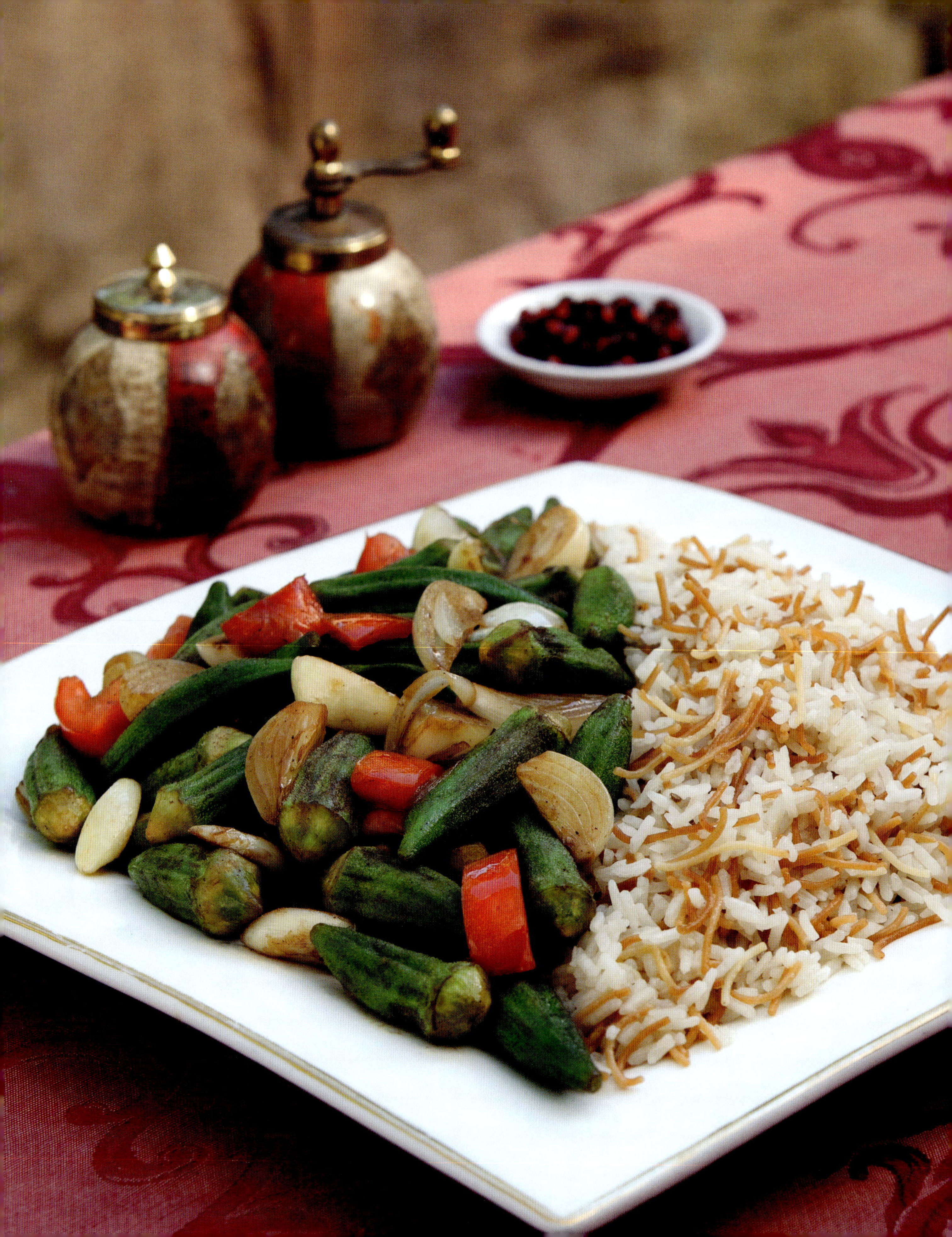

Okra with Rice (vegetarian)

Bamia w'riz

You can also cook bamia with meat, usually lamb.

Heat 2 tablespoons of the olive oil in a saucepan over medium heat, add the okra and fry for a few minutes until they start to change colour. Remove with a slotted spoon and place on paper towel. Add the remaining olive oil to the pan with the onion and garlic and cook until light brown. Add the rest of the ingredients and cook gently for 2 minutes. Add 2 cups water and bring to the boil, then add the okra and reduce the heat to a simmer. Cook for 20 minutes.

Serve with Lebanese rice (see below).

Serves 4–6

3 tablespoons olive oil

500g very small okra, stalks removed, washed and drained

2 large brown onions, sliced

5 cloves garlic, sliced

4 large tomatoes, coarsely chopped

1 teaspoon tomato paste

1 teaspoon salt, or to taste

¼ teaspoon ground black pepper

¼ teaspoon Lebanese mixed spices (see page 12)

2 tablespoons pomegranate molasses

Lebanese Rice

Riz b' sh'airieh

Lebanese rice is very flexible. You can eat it with so many dishes, such as fasoulia, baked kafta, basella or just plain yogurt.

Melt the butter in a small (about 15cm diameter) saucepan over low heat and add the vermicelli. Cook for a few minutes until golden brown, stirring constantly. Stir in the rice and salt and cook for 2 minutes, stirring occasionally. Add 2 cups water and bring to the boil. Reduce the heat to low, cover and simmer for 15 minutes, until the rice is cooked and all the water is absorbed.

Serve immediately.

Serves 4–6

30g unsalted butter

30g egg vermicelli, broken into 10cm pieces

1 cup long grain rice, washed and drained

½ teaspoon salt, or to taste

Chicken and Rice

Riz ala'djaj

- 800g chicken breast fillets
- 1 cinnamon stick
- 2 teaspoons salt, or to taste
- 40g butter
- 1 small brown onion, finely chopped
- 350g coarse lamb mince
- 1½ cups long grain rice, washed and drained
- ½ teaspoon black pepper
- ½ teaspoon Lebanese mixed spices (see page 12)
- 2 tablespoons olive oil
- ½ cup almonds, halved or slivered
- ½ cup pine nuts
- ½ teaspoon ground cinnamon

Place the chicken in a saucepan with 1.5 litres water, the cinnamon stick and 1 teaspoon of the salt. Bring to the boil, removing any scum from the surface. Reduce the heat and simmer for about 20 minutes, until the chicken is cooked. Drain, reserving the stock.

For the rice, place the butter in a non-stick saucepan, add the onion and saute lightly for 5 minutes. Add the lamb and cook for a further 15 minutes, or until the lamb is cooked. Stir in the rice, black pepper, mixed spices and the remaining teaspoon of salt and cook for a few minutes to bring out the rice flavour. Add 3 cups of the reserved chicken stock and bring to the boil, stirring occasionally, then cover, reduce the heat and simmer for 10–12 minutes, until the rice is cooked.

Meanwhile, heat the olive oil in a frying pan over low heat and add the almonds. Cook gently until golden brown, stirring constantly to prevent them burning. Remove with a slotted spoon and set aside. Repeat the process with the pine nuts and add them to the almonds.

To serve, place the rice mixture on a serving platter, shred the chicken fillets and place on top then cover with the pine nut and almond topping. Sprinkle with the ground cinnamon and serve with your favourite salad.

Serves 6

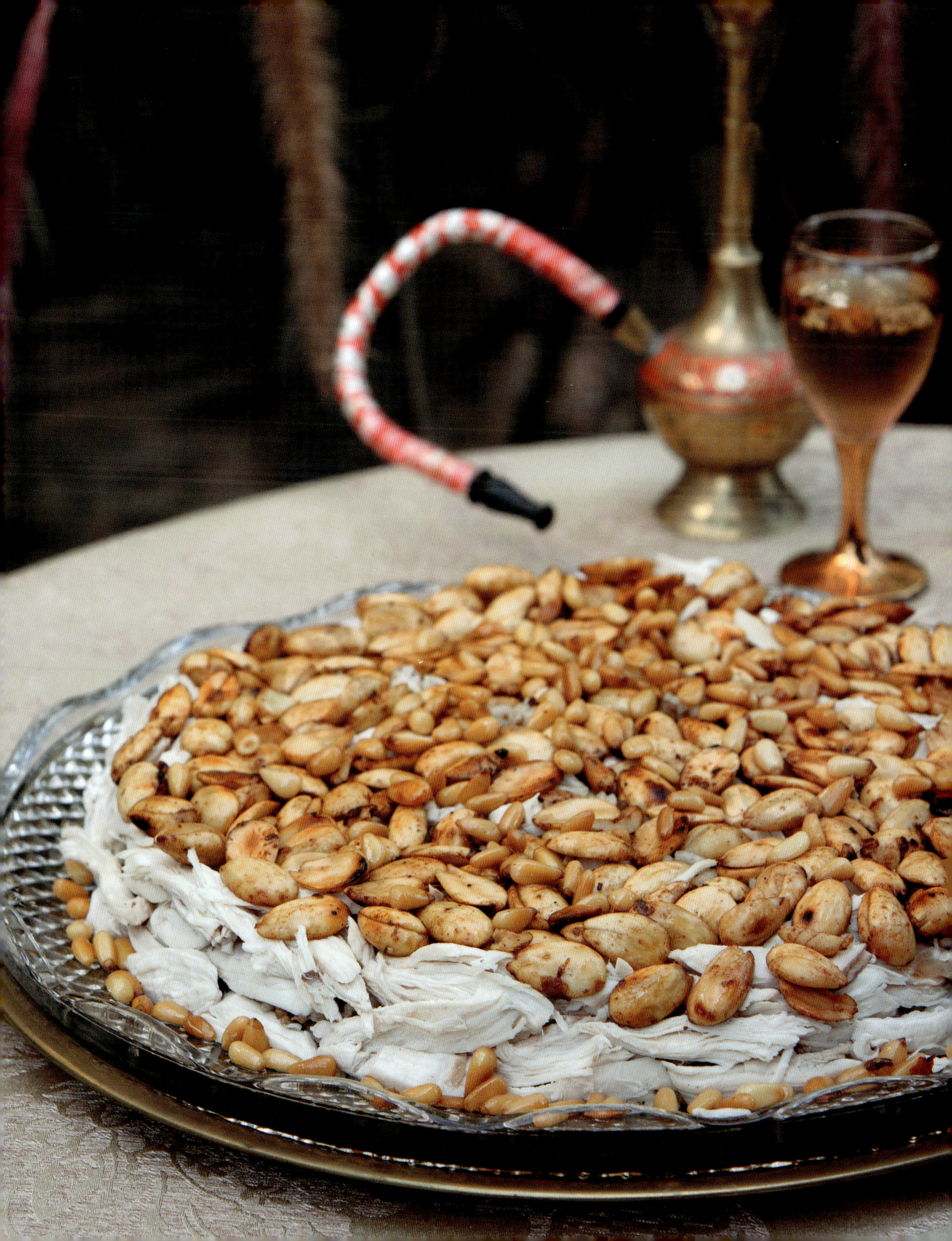

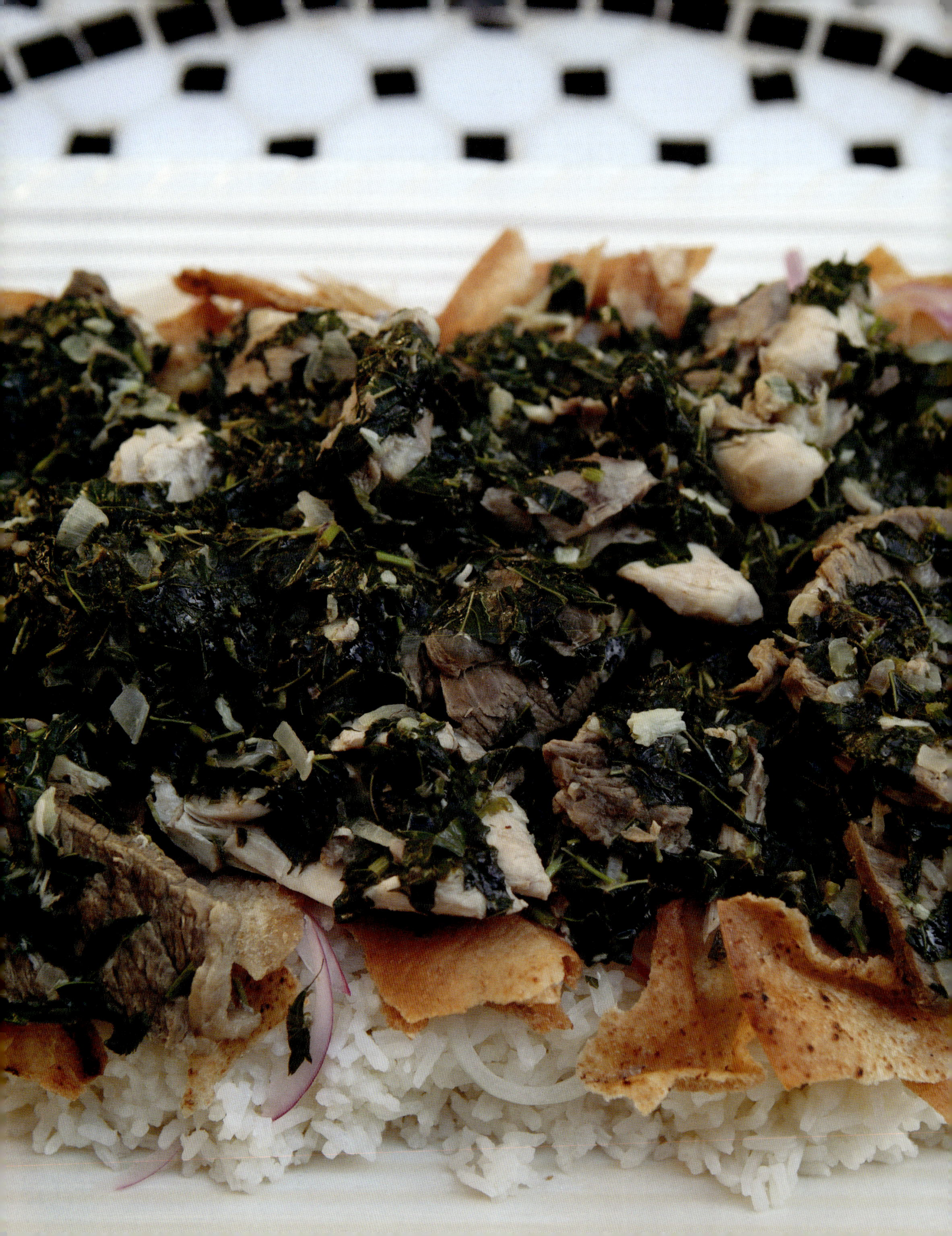

Mouloukia

El mouloukia

In two separate saucepans bring to the boil the lamb chops with 2 litres water and the chicken with 1½ litres water, adding 1 teaspoon salt to each. Reduce the heat and simmer until cooked – 2 hours for the lamb and 1 hour for the chicken – removing any scum from the surface. Remove the meat, combine the two stocks and leave to simmer. Trim the bones from the lamb, cut both the chicken and lamb into bite-sized pieces and keep warm.

For the rice, melt half the butter in a small saucepan, add the rice and cook for 5 minutes, stirring constantly. Add the remaining ½ teaspoon salt and 2 cups water and bring to the boil. Reduce the heat and simmer for 15 minutes, until the rice is cooked. Set aside and keep warm.

For the sauce, place the red onion in a bowl, add the vinegar and mix well with your hand to bruise the onion. Set aside.

Lastly, for the mouloukia, remove the stalks and wash and dry the leaves before chopping finely. Melt the remaining butter in a saucepan over medium heat, add the garlic and chopped onion and cook for 2 minutes. Add the fresh and ground coriander and cook for another 2 minutes, stirring constantly. Add the garlic mixture to the meat stock and bring to the boil. Reduce the heat, add the mouloukia, black pepper and lemon juice and cook for a few minutes (do not overcook as the mouloukia will become bitter). Remove from the heat immediately.

To serve, spoon the rice onto a large serving platter, top with the croutons, then layer with the lamb and chicken, and dress with the onion and vinegar sauce. Spoon the mouloukia over the top and serve immediately.

NOTE: You can also serve each ingredient in a separate dish on the table so everyone can assemble their own.

Serves 6

750g lamb leg chops, trimmed

500g chicken breast fillets

2½ teaspoons salt, or to taste

80g butter

1 cup long grain rice, washed and drained

2 red onions, finely sliced into rings

½ cup white vinegar

1 bunch mouloukia (available at Lebanese shops)

6 cloves garlic, crushed

1 medium brown onion, finely chopped

1 bunch coriander, finely chopped

1 teaspoon ground coriander

½ teaspoon black pepper

¼ cup lemon juice

1 loaf Lebanese bread, cut into 3cm cubes and grilled until crispy

Cabbage Rolls
Mehshi malfouf

1 medium cabbage, outer leaves discarded and 15 leaves carefully removed

8 gloves garlic, sliced

¼ cup lemon juice

1 tablespoon salt, or to taste

¼ cup dried mint

30g butter, chopped

FILLING

1½ cups long grain rice, washed and drained

300g coarse lamb mince

1 teaspoon salt, or to taste

½ teaspoon black pepper

½ teaspoon Lebanese mixed spices (see page 12)

30g butter, melted

In the early days rice was not part of the Lebanese diet. We used crushed wheat or burghul for all our stuffing until rice was introduced and everyone started using it. The poor burghul has taken second place to the rice. There is a Lebanese saying: 'al ez ila el riz oul bourghul shanak halou', which means glory was given to the rice and the burghul hanged himself.

For the filling, place the rice, lamb, salt, black pepper and mixed spices in a bowl. Add the melted butter and mix well with your fingers. Set aside.

Put 2 or 3 cabbage leaves in a pot of simmering water and cook for 1–2 minutes. (If the cabbage leaves are hard to separate from the cabbage, place the whole cabbage in boiling water and then carefully separate each leaf.) Remove and place in a colander to drain. Repeat the process until all the leaves are blanched. Cut each leaf in half lengthways, remove the centre stalk and trim the top. This will make the leaves easier to roll. Line the base of a large saucepan with a few leftover trimmed cabbage leaves.

To roll the cabbage, place one trimmed leaf on a flat surface. Place 1 heaped tablespoon of the filling across the middle of the leaf and spread crossways. Tightly roll the leaf, fold in the sides, and squeeze the roll in the palm of your hand to remove any excess water. Place the roll in the pan. Repeat the process until all the leaves have been used.

Tightly pack the rolls into the pan, side-by-side and layer-by-layer. For extra flavour place a few pieces of sliced garlic between the layers. Pour the lemon juice over the top and add the salt, mint and butter. Pour over just enough water to cover the rolls, then place a heatproof dish or plate on top so the rolls stay secure and tightly packed. Cover the pan with the lid and bring to the boil, then reduce the heat and simmer for 1 hour, or until the rice is cooked.

Serve with plain yoghurt and sprinkle with dried mint.

Makes about 30

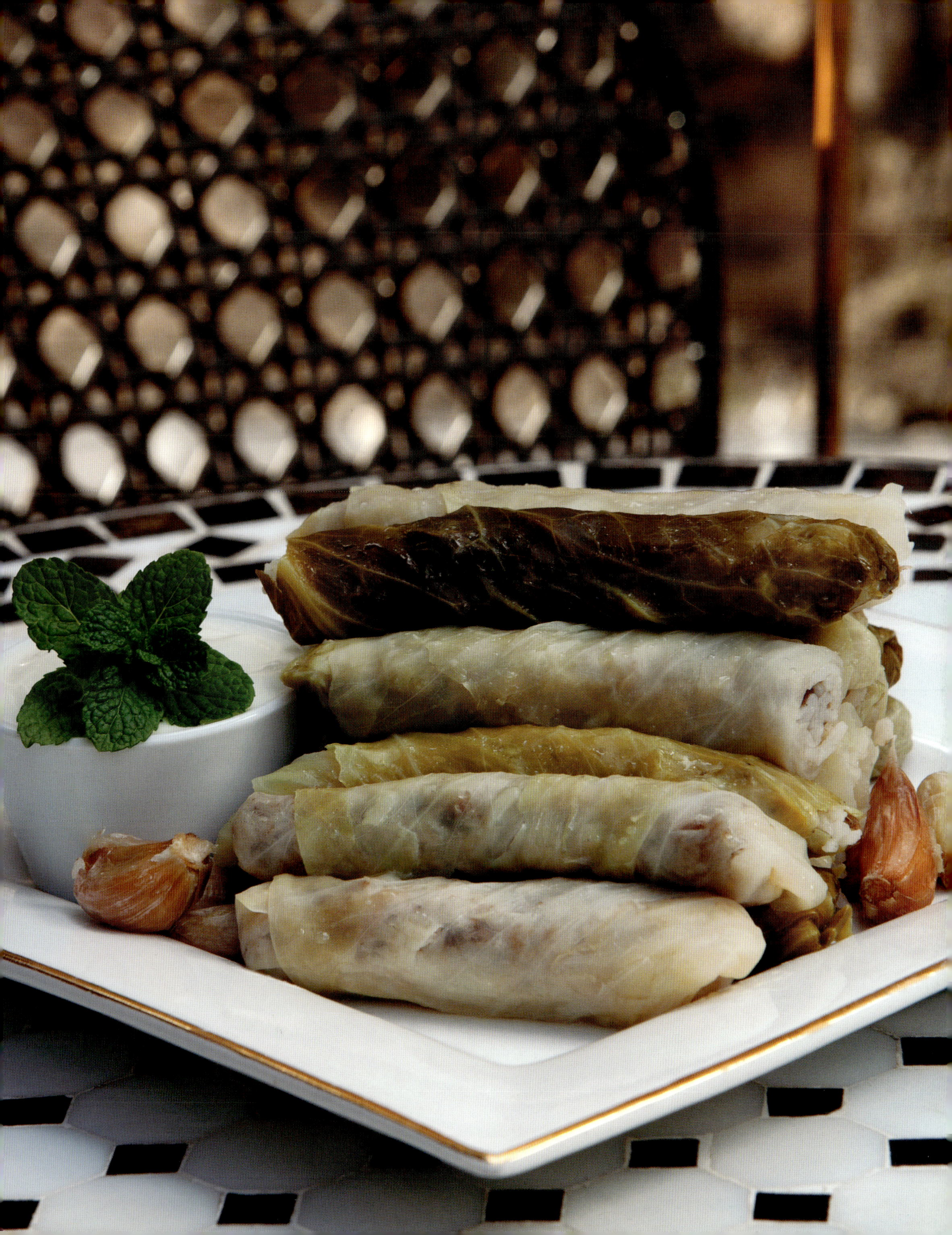

Stuffed Zucchini

Mehshi kousa

- 3 tablespoons tomato paste
- 400g can diced tomatoes
- 2 teaspoons salt, or to taste
- ½ teaspoon black pepper
- 10 small Lebanese zucchini, about 10cm long

STUFFING

- 1 cup long grain rice, washed and drained
- 250g lamb mince
- 30g unsalted butter, melted
- ½ teaspoon salt, or to taste
- ½ teaspoon ground black pepper
- ½ teaspoon Lebanese mixed spices (see page 12)

For the stock, place 1.5 litres water in a saucepan and bring to the boil. Add the tomato paste, tomatoes, salt and black pepper, then reduce the heat and leave to simmer for 20 minutes while you prepare the zucchini.

Trim the stalks off the zucchini and core them (a special corer for zucchini will make this very easy). Remove the pulp to hollow out the zucchini, leaving about an 5mm-thick shell. Place the cored zucchini in a large bowl and wash under cold running water. Drain and set aside.

For the stuffing, place the rice in a bowl, add the lamb, melted butter, salt, black pepper and mixed spices and mix well. Stuff each zucchini shell to about ¾ full, leaving room for the rice to expand. Push the filling in with the handle of a teaspoon to make sure it's well filled. Place the stuffed zucchini and any leftover stuffing in the stock and bring back to the boil. Reduce the heat and simmer for 45 minutes, or until the rice is cooked.

Serve hot with yoghurt.

Makes 10

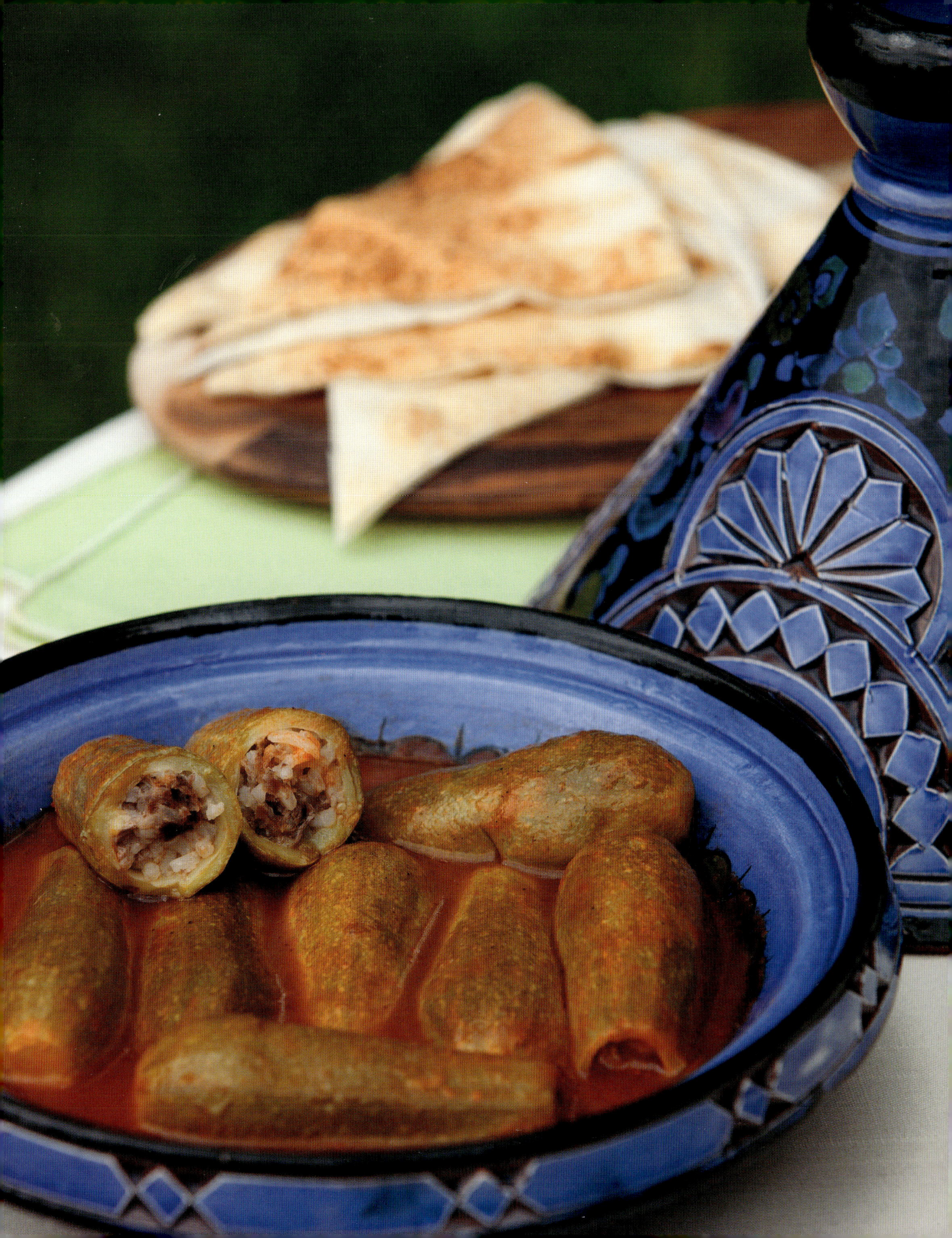

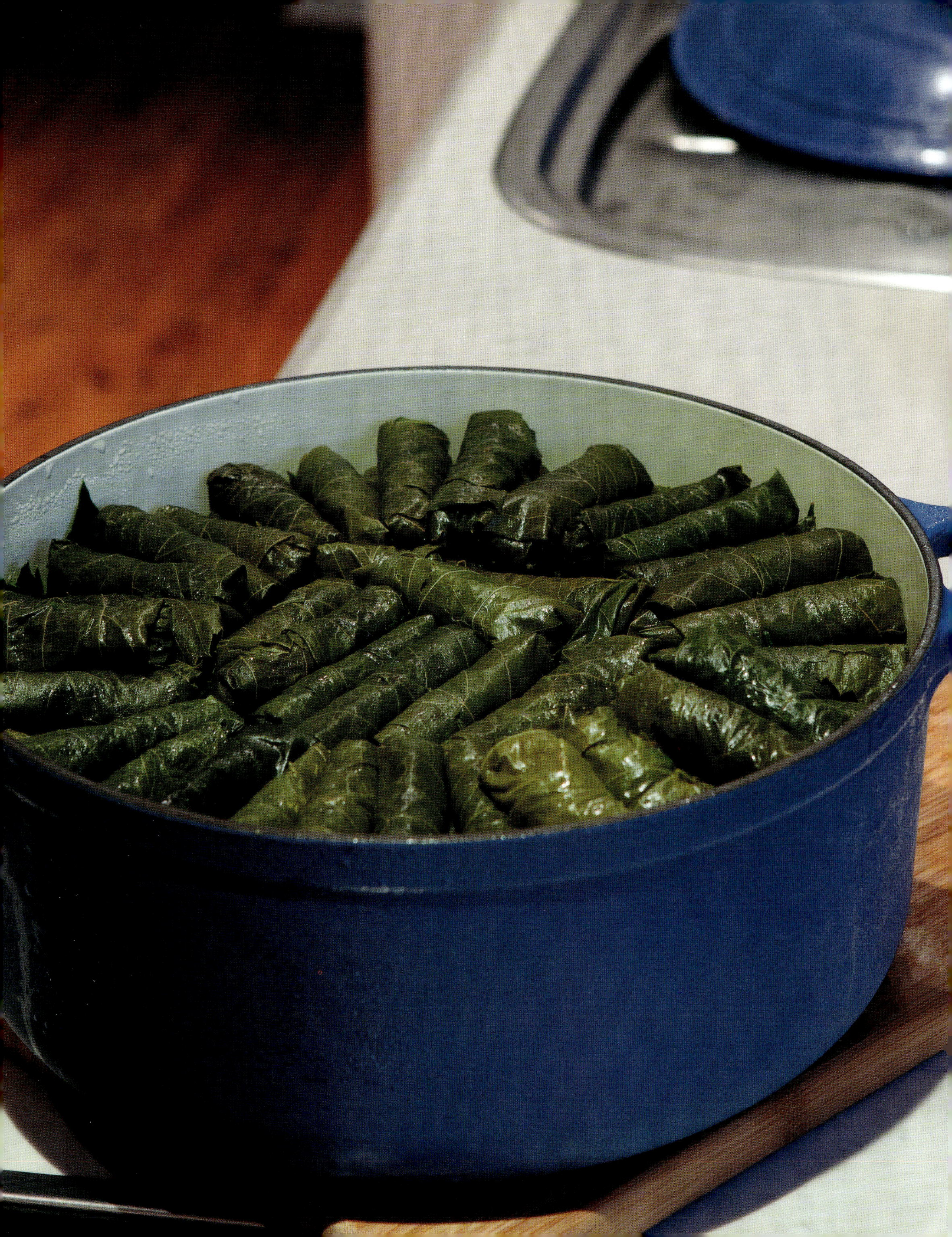

Stuffed Vine Leaves (vegetarian)
Mehshi warak enib oteygh

For the filling, place all the ingredients in a bowl and combine.

Wash and drain the pickled vine leaves or soak the fresh leaves in hot water to wilt. Line the base of a deep, heavy-based saucepan with vine leaves and cover with layers of tomato slices.

Place 1 vine leaf, stalk side up, on a flat board. Add 1 teaspoon of the filling and spread crossways, fold the long sides over and roll the leaf tightly. Place in the saucepan on top of the tomatoes. Repeat the process until the filling is used, packing the stuffed leaves tightly into the saucepan side-by-side and making sure they are very close together.

Sprinkle over the salt, pour in the lemon juice and olive oil and add enough water to cover. Place a heatproof plate on top to prevent the stuffed leaves from floating. Put the lid on the pan, bring to the boil, then reduce the heat to low and simmer for about
1¼ hours, or until the rice is cooked.

Serve with plain yoghurt or as a mezza.

Makes about 50

1kg pickled vine leaves (available at Lebanese or Greek delicatessens), or fresh vine leaves

3 medium tomatoes, cut into 3mm-thick slices

1 tablespoon salt, or to taste

¼ cup lemon juice

¼ cup olive oil

FILLING

1½ cups long grain rice, washed and drained

1 cup chopped tomatoes

2 cups chopped flat-leaf parsley

½ cup finely chopped mint

3 spring onions, finely chopped

¼ cup olive oil

½ teaspoon Lebanese mixed spices (see page 12)

½ teaspoon black pepper

1½ teaspoons salt, or to taste

¼ cup lemon juice

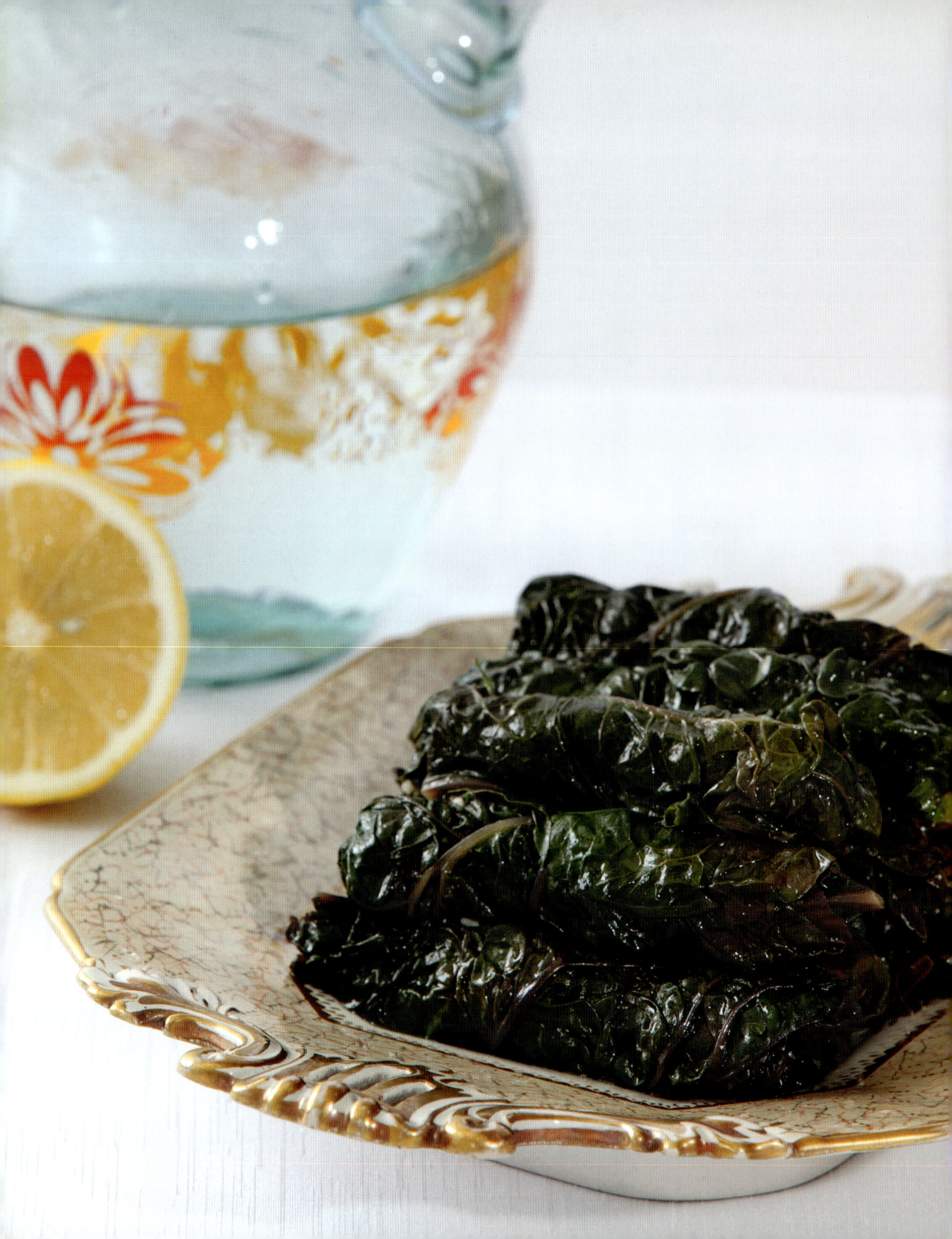

Stuffed Silver Beet (vegetarian)

Mehshi selek

For the filling, place all the ingredients in a bowl and combine.

Cut the silver beet leaves in half so you have pieces measuring about 8cm x 10cm. Smaller leaves can be overlapped to make that size and irregular leaves can be used to line the bottom of the pan. Blanch the leaves in hot water until just wilted and drain under cold running water.

Line the bottom of a deep, heavy-based saucepan with leaves and cover with the tomato slices.

Place 1 leaf on a flat board, add 1 heaped teaspoon of the filling and spread crossways. Fold the sides over and roll up tightly, place in the palm of your hand and squeeze any excess juice into a bowl (this excess juice will be poured over the rolls later). Place in the lined pan in layers, side-by-side, until all the filling is used. Discard any leftover leaves.

Pour the olive oil and lemon juice over the layers and add the salt, then add enough water and the leftover juice to cover the rolled leaves. Place a heatproof dish on the rolls to prevent them floating, cover the pan and bring to the boil. Reduce the heat and simmer for 40 minutes. Set aside to rest for at least 20 minutes before serving.

Serve warm or cold.

Makes about 30

2 bunches silver beet, stalk trimmed

2 medium tomatoes, cut into 5mm-thick slices

¼ cup olive oil

¼ cup lemon juice

1½ teaspoons salt, or to taste

FILLING

1 cup long grain rice, rinsed and drained

½ cup dried split chickpeas, soaked overnight, washed and drained

2 medium tomatoes, finely chopped

3 spring onions, finely chopped

1 cup finely chopped flat-leaf parsley

¼ cup mint, finely chopped

1¼ teaspoons salt, or to taste

½ teaspoon black pepper

½ teaspoon Lebanese mixed spices (see page 12)

¼ cup lemon juice

⅓ cup extra virgin olive oil

Fish with Tahini

Samke harrah

1kg boneless fish fillets, trimmed into 15cm-long pieces

½ tablespoon salt, or to taste

6 gloves garlic, crushed

½ bunch coriander, finely chopped

1 red chilli, finely chopped

½ cup vegetable oil

SAUCE

½ cup tahini paste

½ cup lemon juice

¼ teaspoon salt, or to taste

I grew up in Tripoli and samke harrah is the town's famous dish.

Sprinkle the fish with the salt and set aside for 30 minutes.

Use a mortar and pestle to pound the garlic, coriander and chilli separately and set aside.

Preheat the oven to 180°C.

For the sauce, place the tahini paste in a bowl and add the lemon juice and salt. Slowly add 1½ cups water, stirring constantly, to form a thin sauce. Set aside.

Heat the oil in a non-stick frying pan until very hot. Add the fish and fry for 2 minutes on each side, then remove with a slotted spoon and transfer to a baking tray.

In the same oil, fry the garlic until it changes colour. Add the coriander and the chilli, cook for 1 minute, then add the tahini sauce and stir well. Pour over the fish, cover with aluminium foil and bake for 30 minutes.

Serve hot or cold.

NOTE: If you wish, you can use a whole fish rather than fillets. Clean the fish before salting.

Serves 4

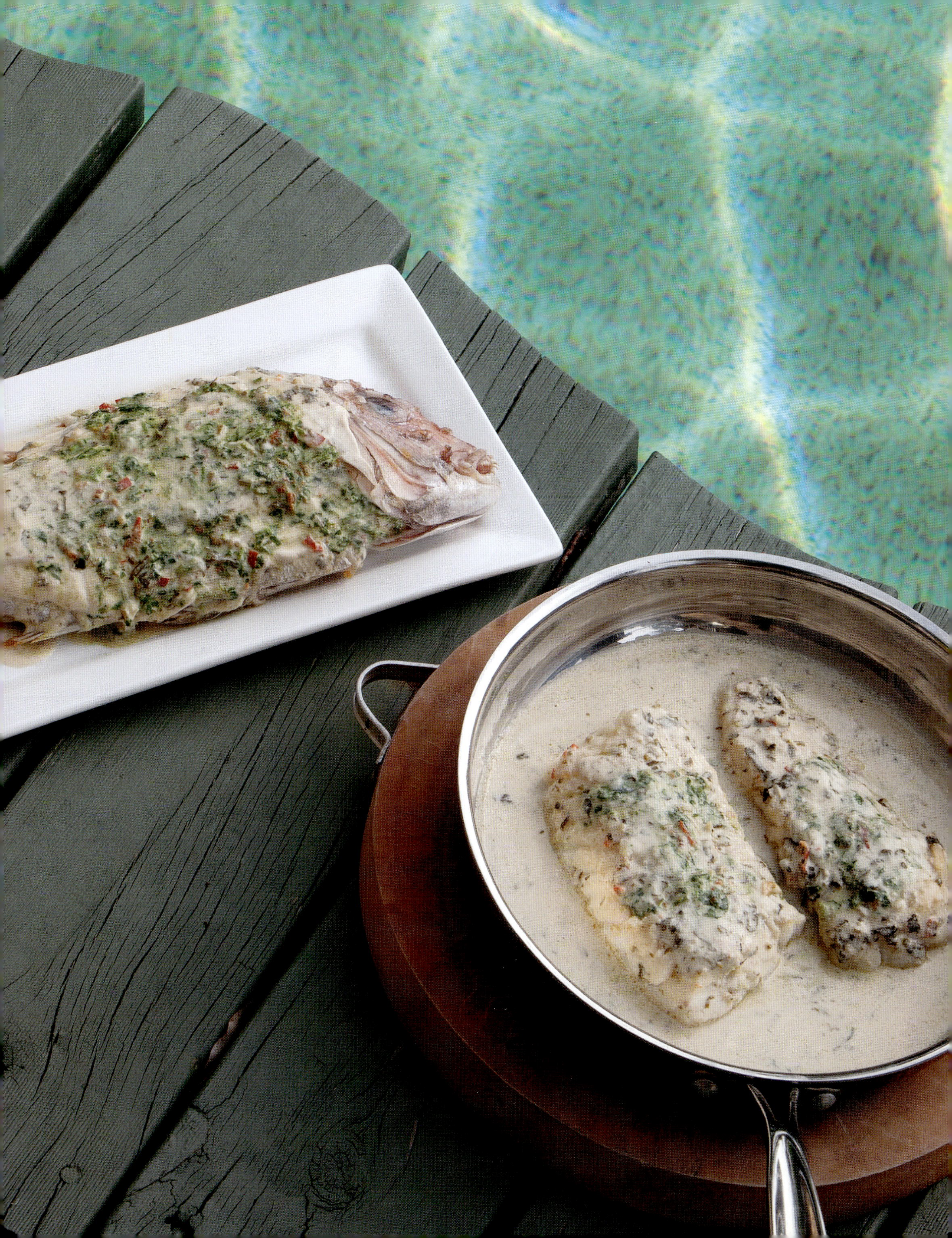

Grilled Fish

Samak meshwi

1 whole snapper or barramundi (about 1kg)

½ teaspoon salt, or to taste

¼ cup olive oil

pinch paprika, to garnish

SAUCE

½ cup tahini paste

2 cloves garlic, crushed

¼ cup lemon juice

½ teaspoon salt, or to taste

1 cup flat-leaf parsley, finely chopped

Clean the fish, sprinkle with the salt and set aside for 30 minutes.

For the sauce, place the tahini paste, garlic, lemon juice and salt in a bowl and combine. Add ½ cup water, stirring constantly, to form a thick sauce. Add the parsley and mix well. Set aside.

Place a length of baking paper over aluminium foil and position the fish in the centre. Add the oil and rub over the fish. Wrap tightly so no air can escape and place on a baking tray. Place the tray under a heated grill and cook for 15 minutes on each side, or you can barbecue the fish until cooked.

Carefully unwrap the foil and baking paper, keeping the fish whole, and transfer to a serving platter. Pour over the tahini sauce, sprinkle with paprika and garnish with extra parsley if you wish.

Serve hot or cold with your favourite salad.

Serves 4

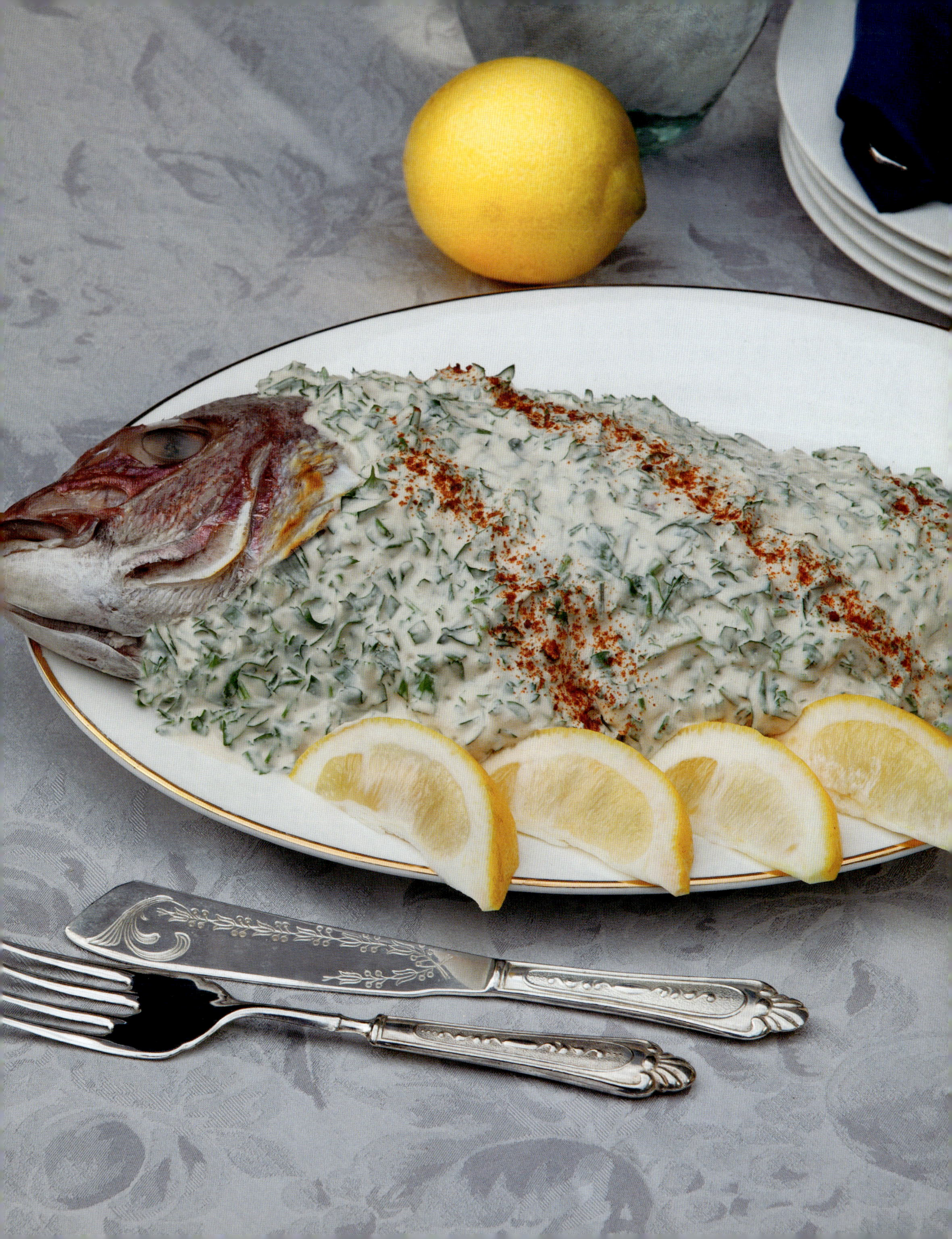

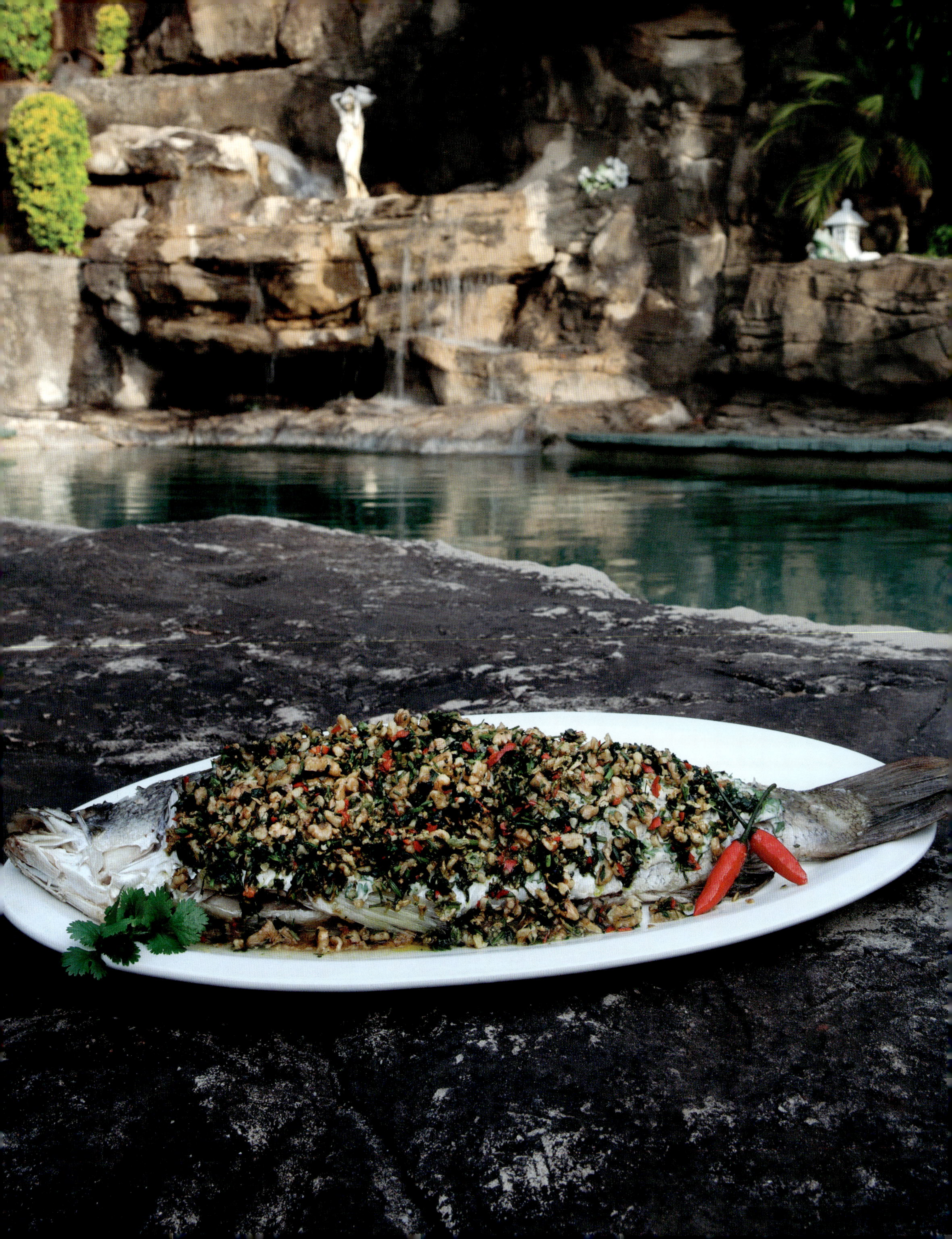

Baked Fish with Walnuts
Samak bil'joz

This dish is served at special functions. Every cook makes their own version.

Clean the fish, sprinkle with the salt and set aside for 30 minutes. Preheat the oven to 180°C and line a baking tray with baking paper.

For the sauce, place the tahini paste in a bowl, add the salt and lemon juice and gradually add enough water, stirring constantly, to form a thick sauce. Set aside.

Place the fish on the prepared tray and rub with the olive oil. Wrap in the paper, folding in the sides, and bake for 20 minutes.

Meanwhile, for the walnut dressing, use a mortar and pestle to pound the garlic, coriander and chilli separately and set aside. Place the olive oil in a frying pan, add the garlic and cook for 1 minute. Add the coriander and chilli and cook until the coriander is crunchy. Remove from heat and stir in the walnuts.

Remove the fish from the oven, unwrap the baking paper and carefully peel off the skin, leaving the head and tail intact (to look good on the serving platter). Spread with the sauce and the walnut dressing, leaving the head and tail uncovered.

Serve warm or cold.

Serves 4

1 whole snapper or barramundi (about 1kg), or 1kg fillets

1 teaspoon salt, or to taste

1 tablespoon olive oil

SAUCE

¼ cup tahini paste

¼ teaspoon salt, or to taste

2 tablespoons lemon juice

WALNUT DRESSING

4 cloves garlic, crushed

1 bunch coriander, finely chopped

2 small red chillies, finely chopped

2 tablespoons olive oil

½ cup crushed walnuts

Lentil Soup or Monk Soup (vegetarian)

Kibbet el'rahib

- 2 cups green lentils
- 2 cups finely chopped silver beet, green part only
- 5 cloves garlic, crushed
- ¼ cup olive oil
- ½ cup lemon juice
- 1 teaspoon salt, or to taste

DUMPLINGS
- ¾ cup burghul (crushed wheat)
- 1 small brown onion, grated
- ¼ cup chopped mint
- 1 teaspoon salt, or to taste
- ½ teaspoon black pepper
- ½ teaspoon Lebanese mixed spices (see page 12)
- ¾ cup plain flour

This soup is part of Good Friday's menu.

For the dumplings, soak the burghul in cold water for 20 minutes then drain. Pound the onion, mint, salt, black pepper and mixed spices in a mortar and pestle until fine. Place the burghul in a bowl, add the ground ingredients and the flour and mix well, adding enough water (about ½ cup) to form a dough-like consistency. Wet your hands and make small balls of about ½ teaspoon of the mixture and place them on a tray. Repeat the process until all the mixture is used.

Place the lentils in a large saucepan with 4 cups water and bring to the boil over medium–high heat. Cook for 10 minutes, removing any scum from the surface. Add 1 cup water to prevent the lentils rising to the surface and cook for 10–15 minutes, until the lentils are tender.

Add the dumplings, chopped silver beet, garlic, olive oil, lemon juice and salt and cook over low heat for 15 minutes.

Serve hot with Lebanese bread.

Serves 4–6

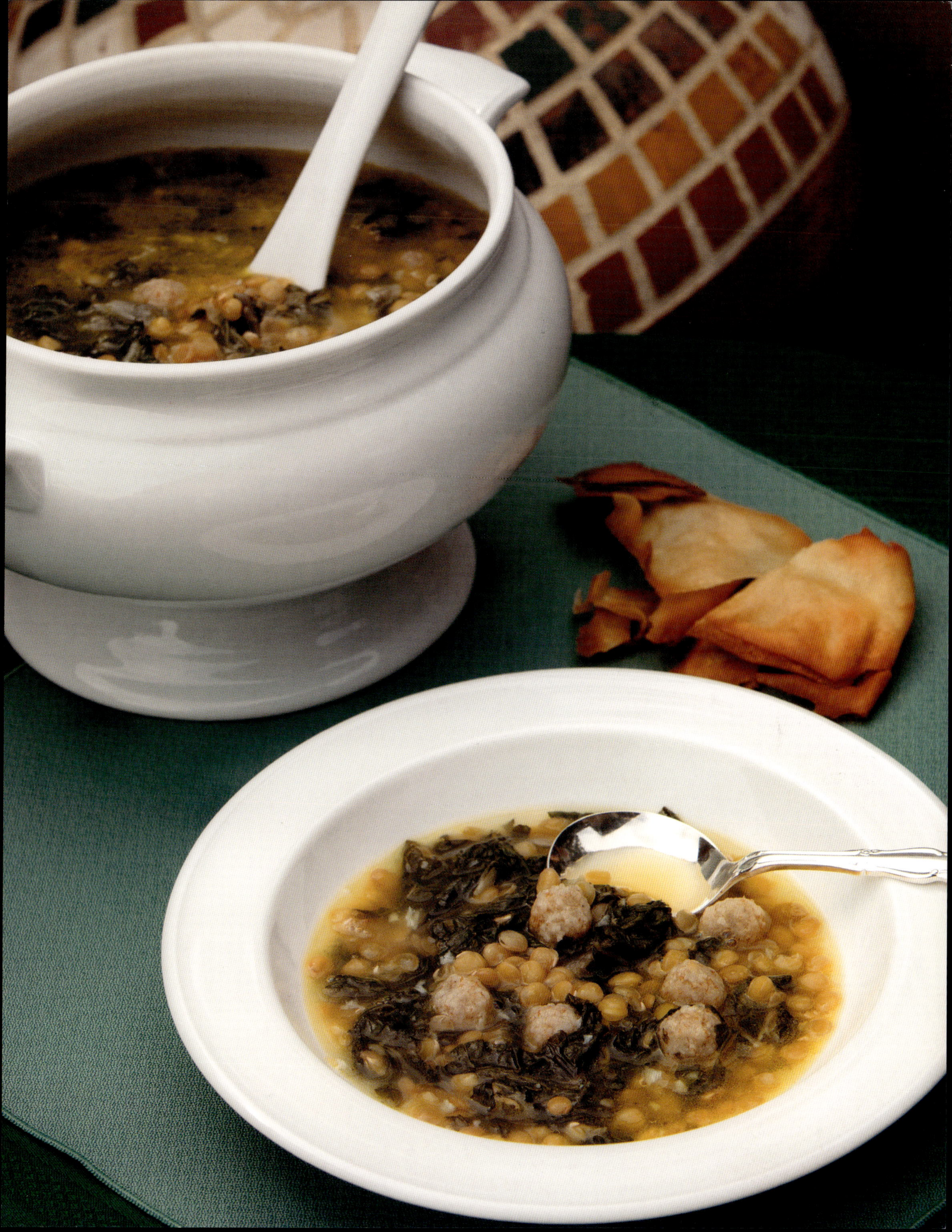

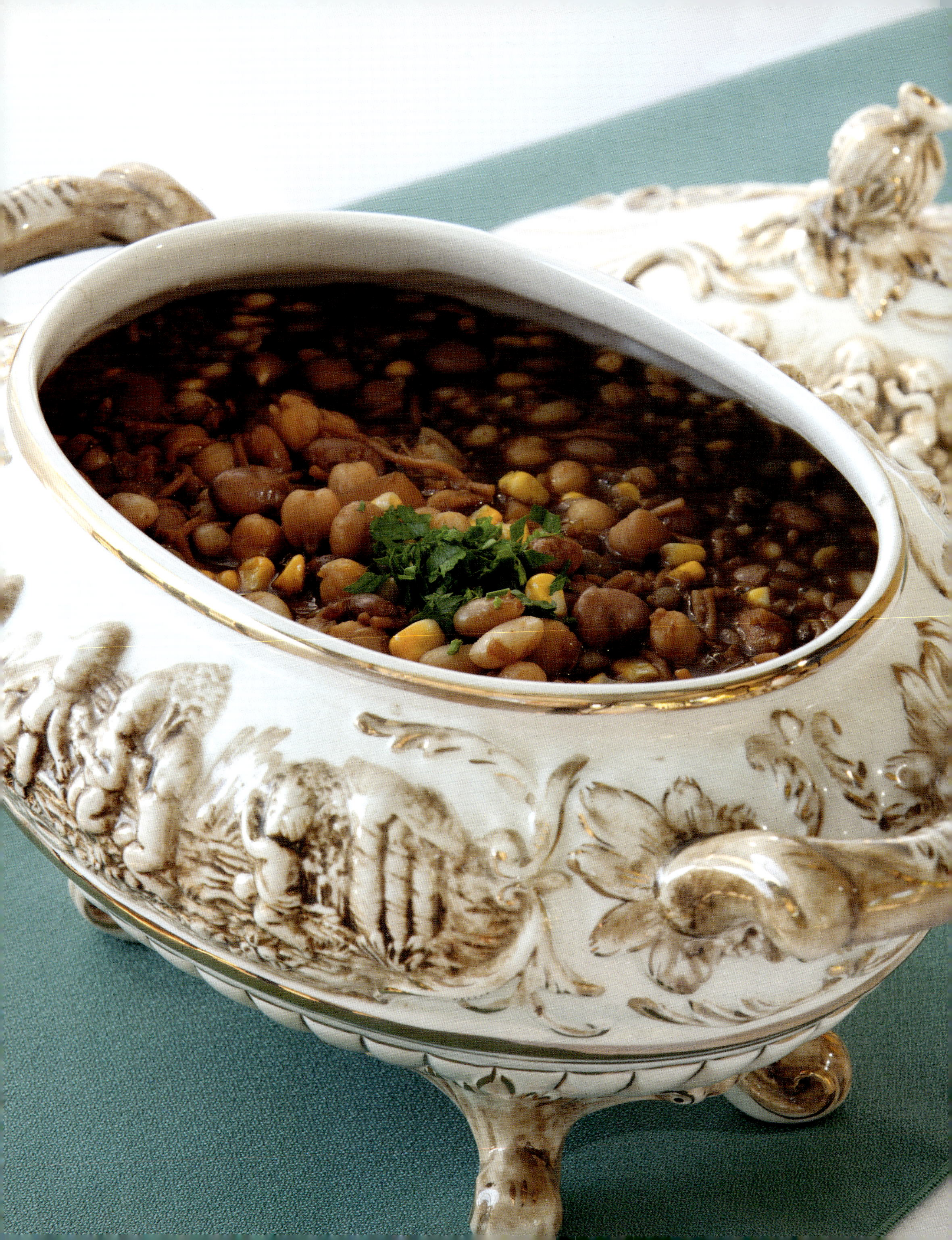

Mixed Legumes Soup (vegetarian)
Maklouta

When I was a child we always had maklouta in winter. My father believed this soup gave us energy and promoted wellbeing.

Soak the chickpeas, barley, kidney beans and butter beans together in water overnight.

The next day, drain the water then wash the legumes and barley and place in a large saucepan with 5 cups water. Bring to the boil, then reduce the heat and simmer for 20 minutes, skimming off any scum. Add the lentils and cook for a further 10 minutes, then add 2 cups water to prevent the lentils floating and continue cooking.

Meanwhile, heat the oil in saucepan over medium heat, add the onion and cook gently until golden brown. Ladle 1 cup of liquid from the soup mixture over the onion to soften it. Add the onion and oil to the soup mixture and stir well. Add the potatoes, burghul or rice, salt, noodles and the tomato and corn if using. Cover the pan and simmer gently over low heat for 1 hour, until the soup is thick. (Everything should be covered with water. Top up with boiling water if you like your soup thin.)

Serve hot with Lebanese bread.

Serves 6–8

1 cup dried chickpeas, washed and drained

½ cup barley, washed and drained

½ cup dried red kidney beans, washed and drained

½ cup dried butter beans, washed and drained

½ cup brown lentils, washed and drained

½ cup olive oil

2 large brown onions, finely chopped

2 medium potatoes, cut into 1cm cubes

¼ cup coarse burghul (crushed wheat) or rice, washed and drained

1 tablespoon salt, or to taste

handful vermicelli noodles

400g can diced tomatoes (optional)

¼ cup frozen corn (optional)

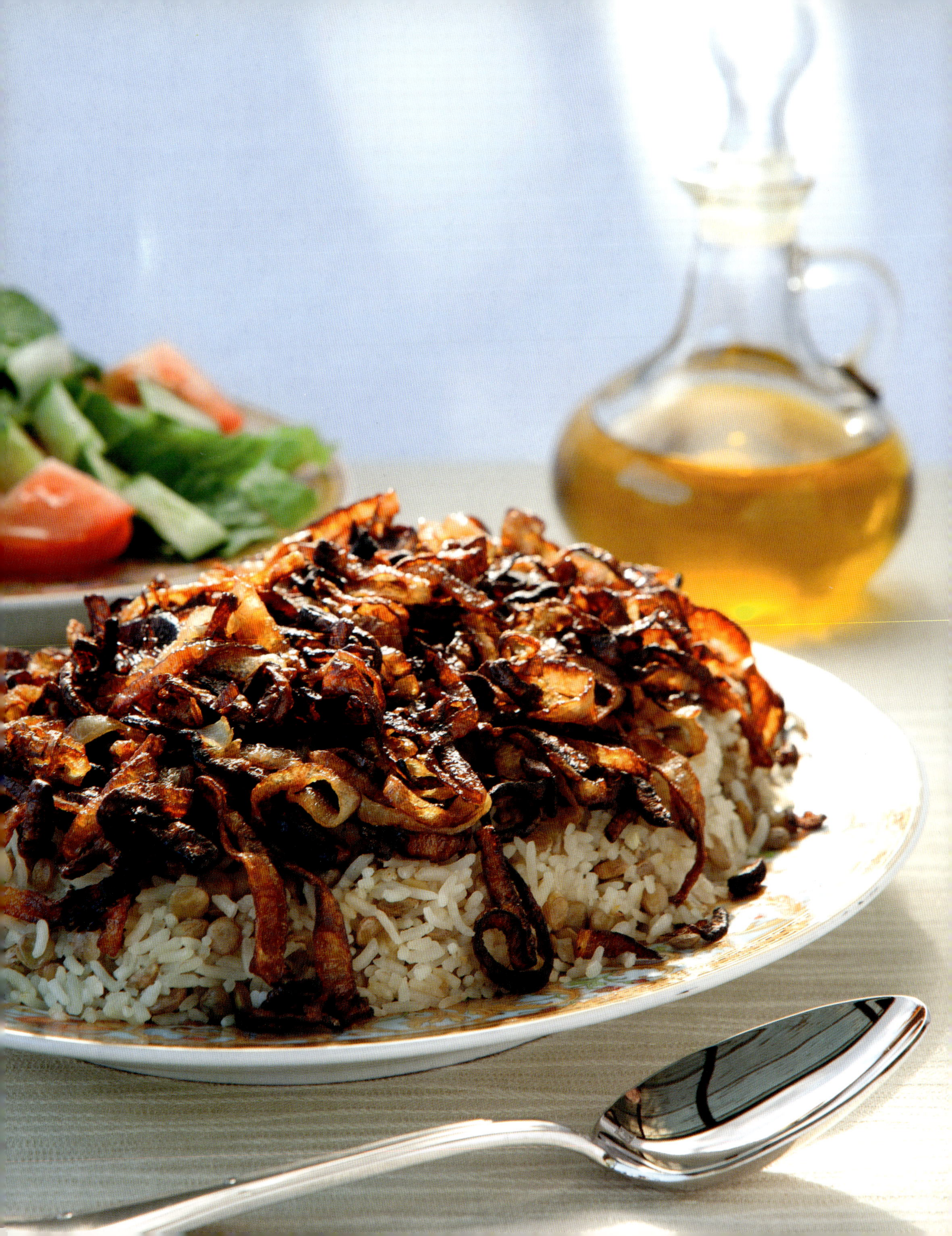

Lentils with Rice (vegetarian)

Mjadra mdradrah

Place the lentils and 3 cups water in a saucepan and bring to the boil, removing any scum from the surface. Add another 2 cups cold water to prevent the lentils splitting and cook over medium heat for 10 minutes. Drain and set aside, reserving the liquid.

Heat 3 tablespoons of the olive oil in the same pan and cook the sliced onion over medium heat until golden. Remove with a slotted spoon and set aside. Add the remaining olive oil and the chopped onion to the pan and cook for 5 minutes, or until lightly brown. Add the rice and drained lentils and cook for at least 3 minutes, stirring constantly to prevent it sticking. Add the salt and 2½ cups of the reserved liquid and bring to the boil. Reduce the heat, cover and simmer for 15 minutes, until all the water has evaporated or the rice is cooked.

Spoon the rice and lentils onto a serving plate, cover with the onion slices and serve with a garden salad.

Serves 4–6

1½ cups green lentils, washed and drained

4 tablespoons olive oil

3 medium brown onions, sliced lengthways

1 small brown onion, finely chopped

¾ cup long grain rice, washed and drained

1½ teaspoons salt, or to taste

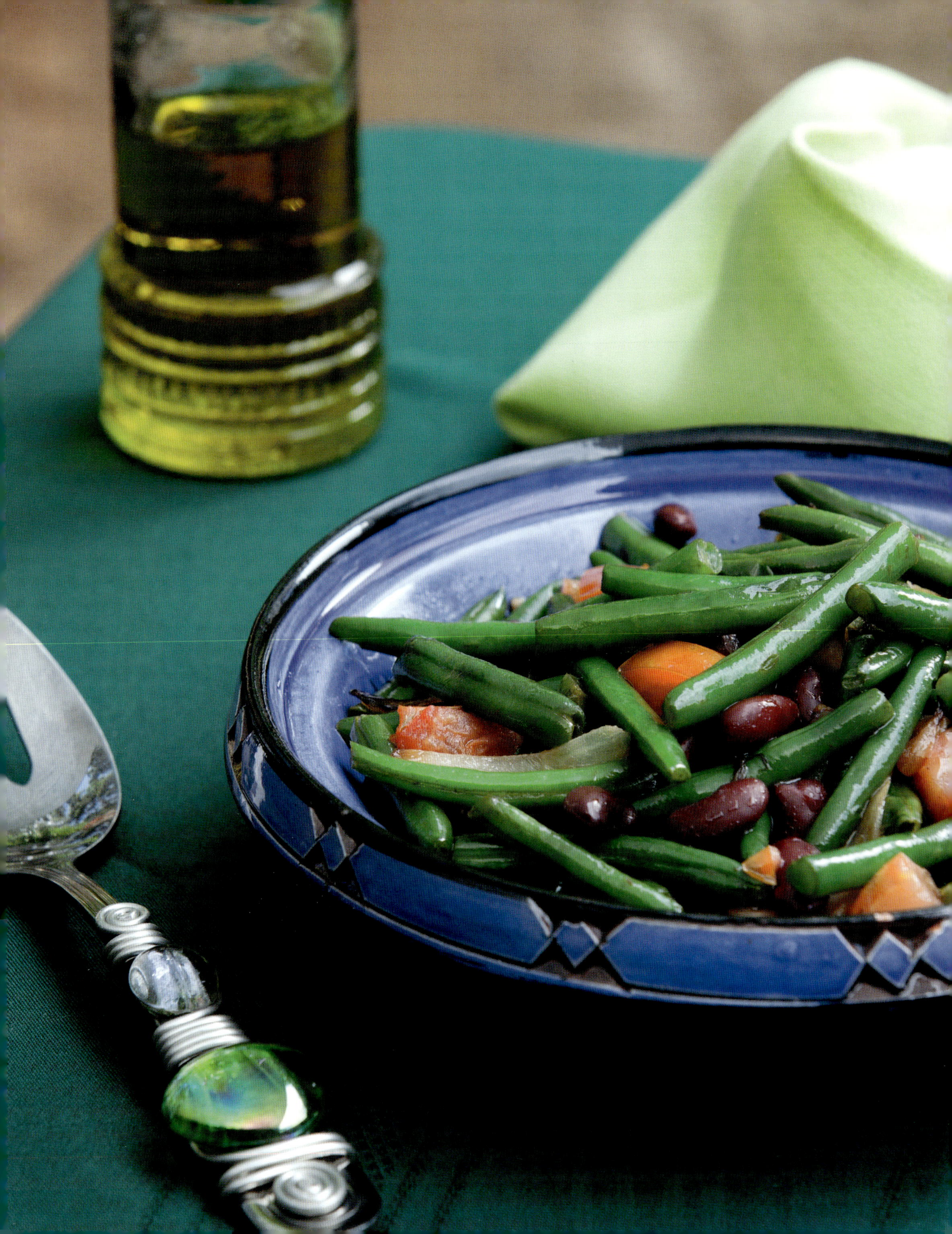

Green Beans with Oil (vegetarian)

Loubia b'zaait

Heat the olive oil in a saucepan over high heat, add the onion and garlic and cook for a few minutes, until golden. Add the green beans and the salt, reduce the heat to medium and cook for 8 minutes, stirring occasionally. Add the tomato, reduce the heat to low and cover and simmer for 15 minutes. Add the red kidney beans, white pepper and mixed spices and cook for a further 5–10 minutes.

Serve warm or cold with a garden salad or your favourite meat.

Serves 4

¼ cup olive oil

2 large brown onions, finely chopped

3 cloves garlic, crushed

1kg green stringless beans, trimmed and halved lengthways

1½ teaspoons salt, or to taste

4 medium tomatoes, chopped

400g can red kidney beans, washed and drained

¼ teaspoon white pepper

¼ teaspoon Lebanese mixed spices (see page 12)

Falafel (vegetarian)
El falafel

300g dried chickpeas

300g split broad beans

2 teaspoons bicarbonate of soda

½ cup chopped flat-leaf parsley

1 bunch coriander, chopped

1 large brown onion, chopped

8 gloves garlic, chopped

2 red chillies, chopped

¼ cup chopped mint

1 tablespoon salt, or to taste

1 teaspoon black pepper

1 teaspoon Lebanese mixed spices (see page 12)

1 tablespoon ground cumin

vegetable oil, for deep-frying

SAUCE

½ cup tahini paste

½ teaspoon salt, or to taste

¼ cup lemon juice

I used to buy falafel on my way home from school. The falafel stand in Lebanon is like the hot dog stand in New York, there was one on every corner. The falafel roll is not only delicious but also good for you, and very easy to make.

For the sauce, place the tahini paste in a bowl, add the salt and slowly stir in the lemon juice and ½ cup water until smooth. Set aside.

Soak the chickpeas and broad beans in 5 cups water and 1 teaspoon bicarbonate of soda overnight. Drain and rinse.

Place the chickpeas, broad beans, parsley, coriander, onion, garlic, chilli and mint in a food processor and blend to a coarse couscous-like texture. (For the best consistency, put through a hand-mincer fitted with a medium blade.) Transfer to a bowl, add the salt, black pepper and spices and mix well until combined.

Add the remaining bicarbonate of soda and combine, then shape the mixture into balls about the size of a golf ball, or press the mixture into a falafel mould.

Heat the vegetable oil until hot and deep-fry the falafels in batches until golden brown. Remove and drain on paper towel.

Serve with the tahini sauce, and accompany with sliced tomato, sliced cucumber and pickled turnip (available at Lebanese shops).

NOTE: The falafel mixture can be frozen and kept for 2 months, or stored in the fridge for 1 week.

Makes 28

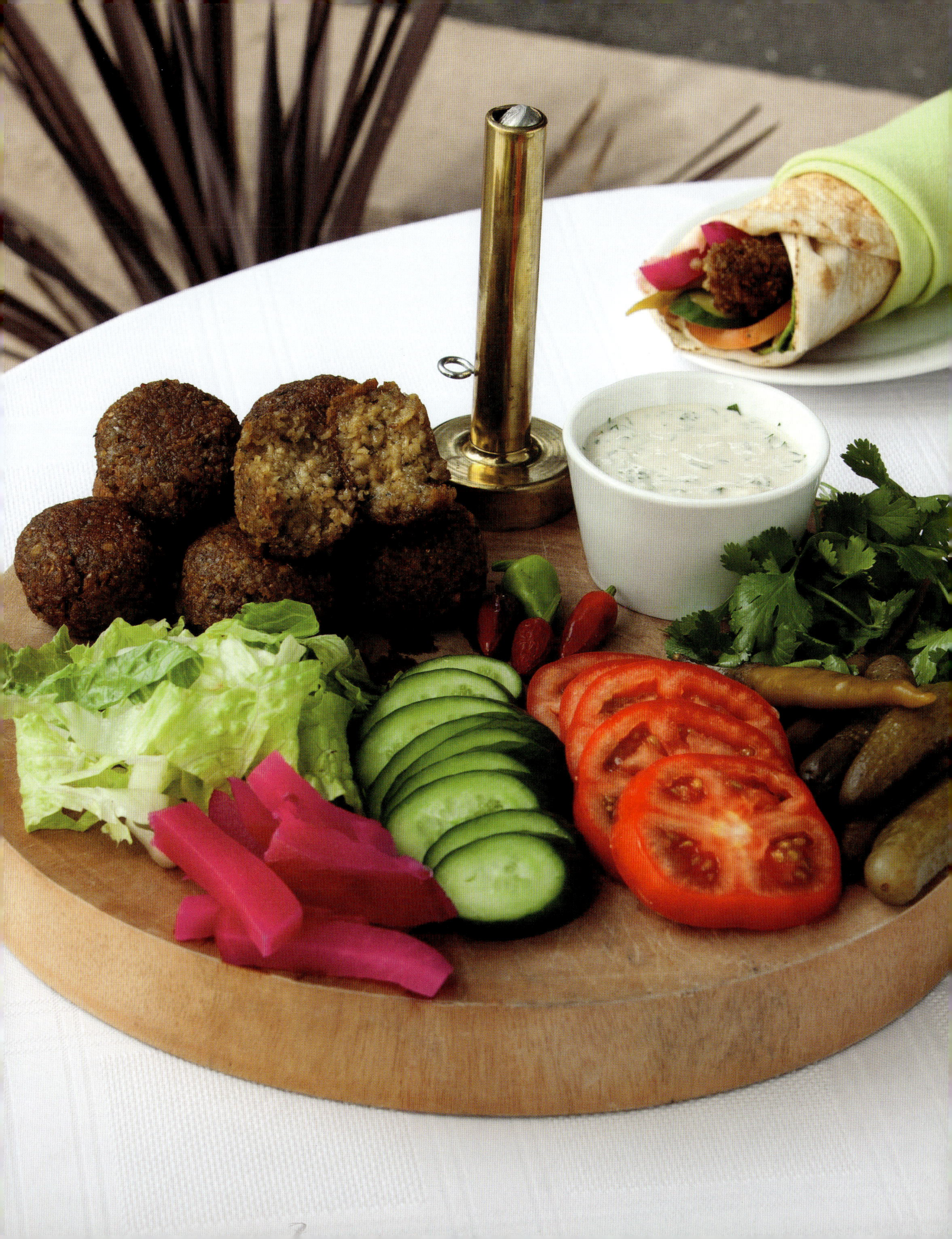

Fried Eggplant (vegetarian)

Batingane Maq'ley

2 medium eggplants

1 tablespoon salt, or to taste

½ cup plain flour

2 cups canola oil, for frying

SAUCE

5 cloves garlic, chopped

½ teaspoon salt, or to taste

¼ cup olive oil

¼ cup lemon juice

For the sauce, place the garlic and salt in a mortar and pestle and pound thoroughly. Gradually work in the olive oil and the lemon juice, pounding constantly. Set aside.

Slice the eggplants crossways into 1cm-thick rounds. Cover with cold water and set aside for 1 hour.

Drain, sprinkle with the salt, pat dry and dust in the flour.

Heat the oil in a non-stick frying pan and fry the eggplant for 4 minutes on each side (you can fry in batches depending on the size of the pan). Remove and place on paper towel to drain. Repeat the process until all the eggplant is cooked.

Serve hot or cold with the sauce as a mezza.

NOTE: See over the page for picture.

Mezza

Pan-fried Cauliflower (vegetarian)

Arnabit maq'ley

For the sauce, place the garlic in a bowl, add the tahini paste and the salt then gradually add the lemon juice and ¼ cup water, stirring constantly until you have a smooth consistency (add more water if needed). Set aside.

Place 4 cups water in a deep saucepan and bring to the boil. Drop in the cauliflower, making sure there is enough water to cover, and boil for 5 minutes. Drain in a colander and set aside until cold.

Heat the oil in a deep frying pan until hot. Fry the cauliflower in batches until golden brown, then remove with a slotted spoon and place on paper towel to drain. Repeat until all the cauliflower is cooked.

Serve hot or cold with the tahini sauce (pictured at the top of page 24)
as a mezza.

NOTE: See over the page for picture.

Mezza

1 medium cauliflower, broken into florets

2 cups canola oil, for frying

SAUCE

1 clove garlic, crushed

½ cup tahini paste

¼ teaspoon salt, or to taste

2 tablespoons lemon juice

Potato Wedges (vegetarian)

Patata maq'ley

Fried vegetables are always on the Lebanese table as a side dish or mezza.

For the sauce, place the garlic and salt in mortar and pestle and pound to combine. Gradually add the olive oil and the lemon juice, pounding constantly until finished.

Peel the potatoes, cut into wedges about 2cm thick and sprinkle with the salt. Heat the oil in a deep frying pan until very hot and add as many wedges as will fit in the pan. Cook for about 10 minutes, until light golden. Remove with a slotted spoon and place on paper towel. Repeat until all the wedges are cooked.

Serve hot with the sauce as a mezza.

Mezza

6 medium potatoes (such as desiree)

1 teaspoon salt, or to taste

2 cups canola oil, for frying

SAUCE

5 cloves garlic, chopped

½ teaspoon salt, or to taste

¼ cup olive oil

¼ cup lemon juice

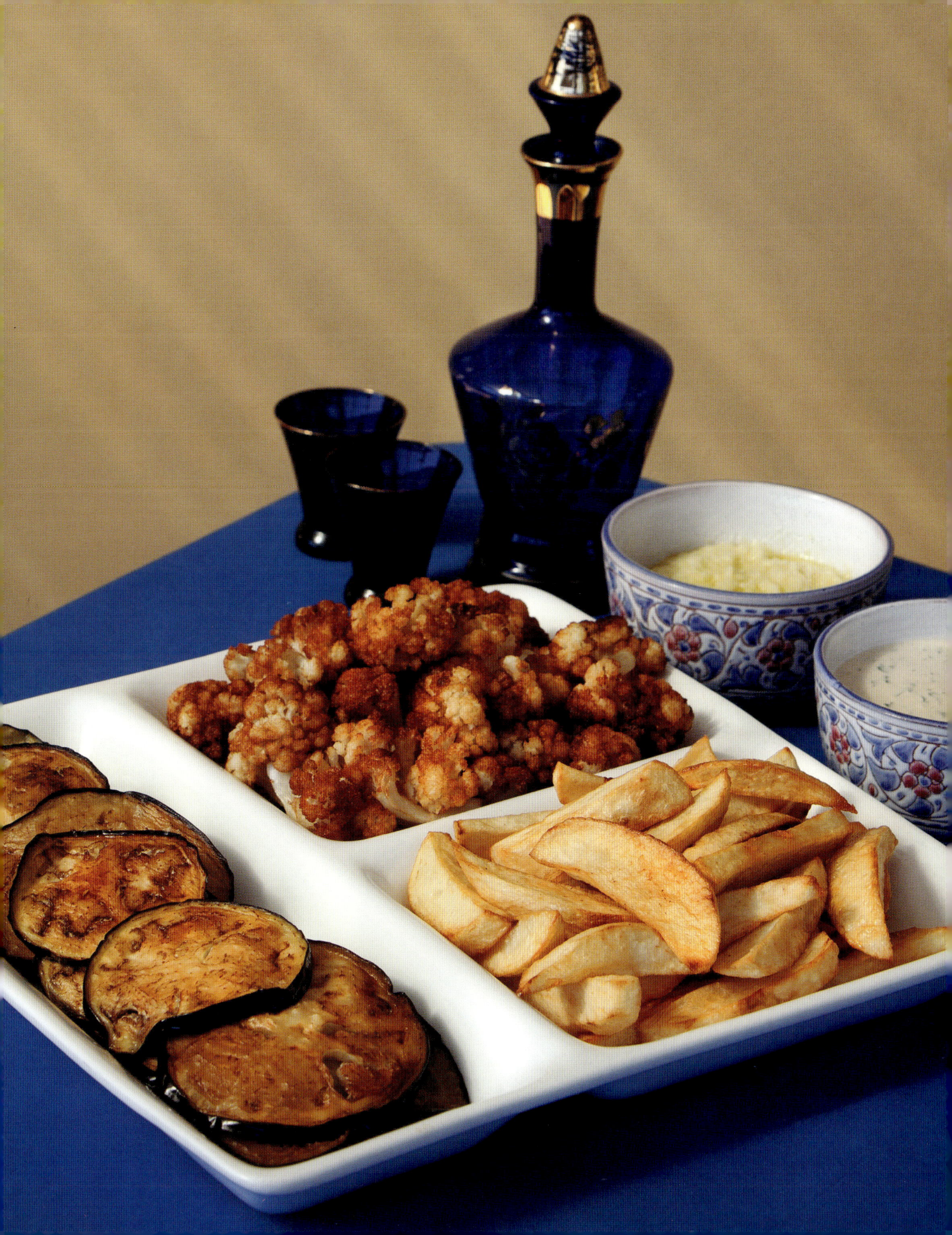

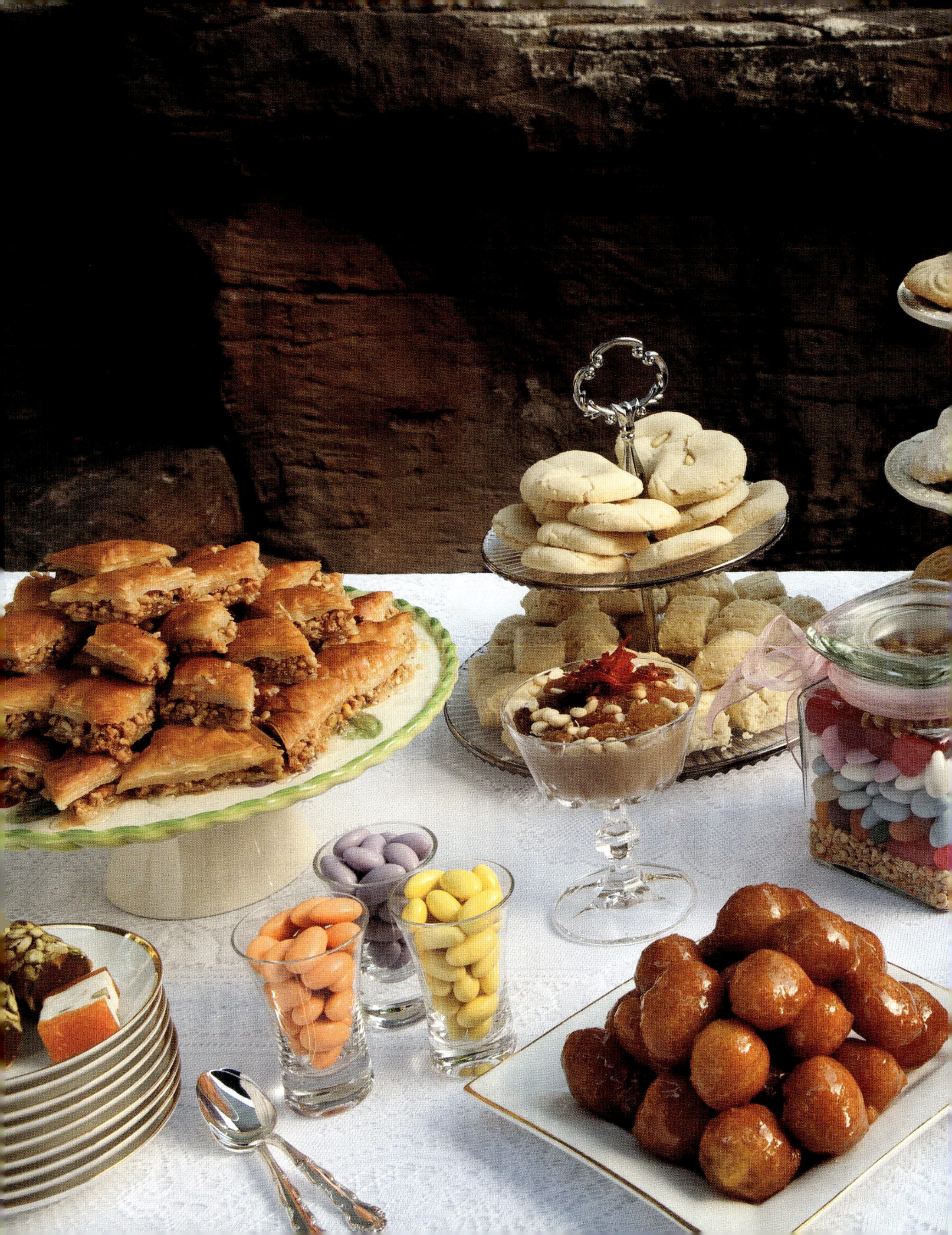

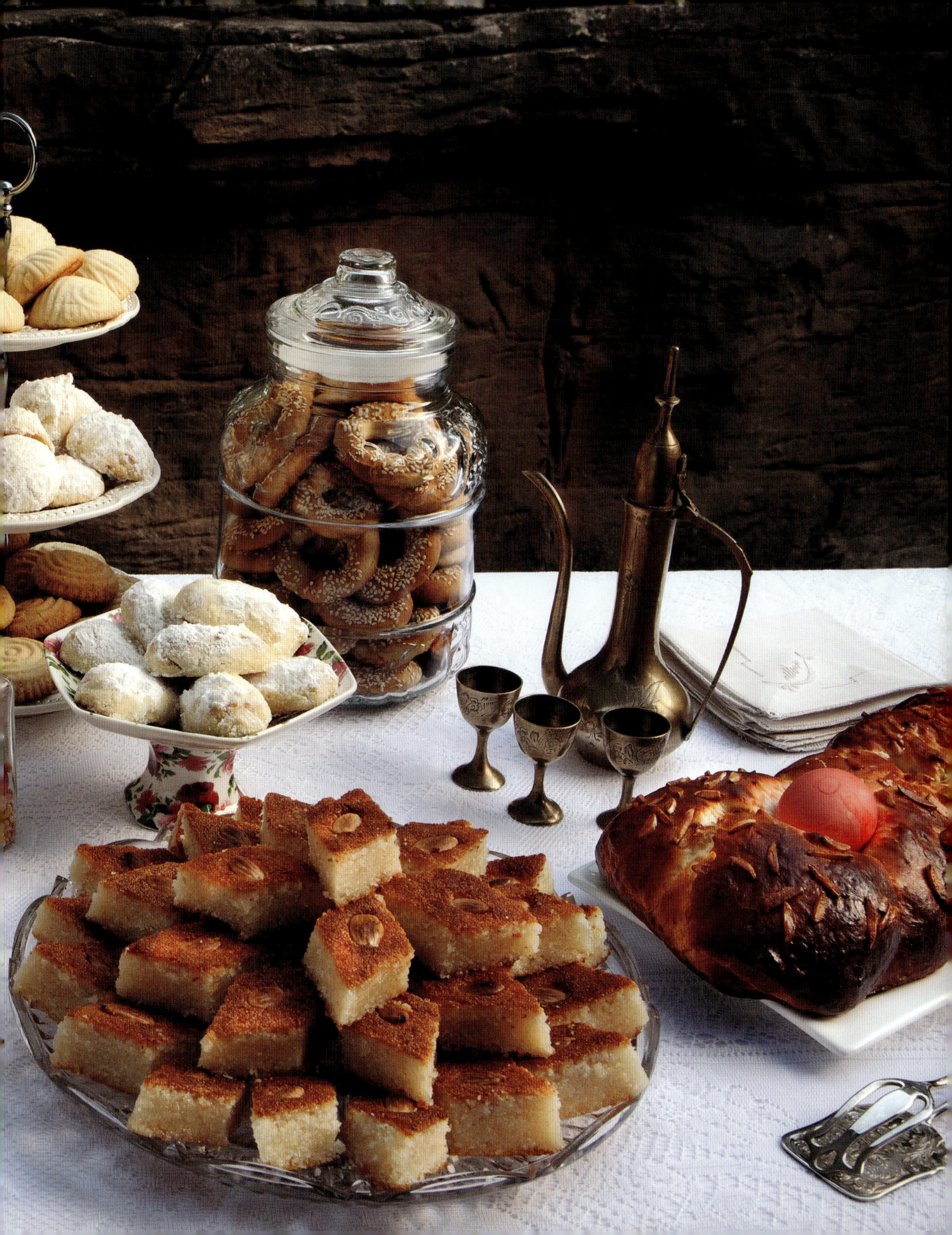

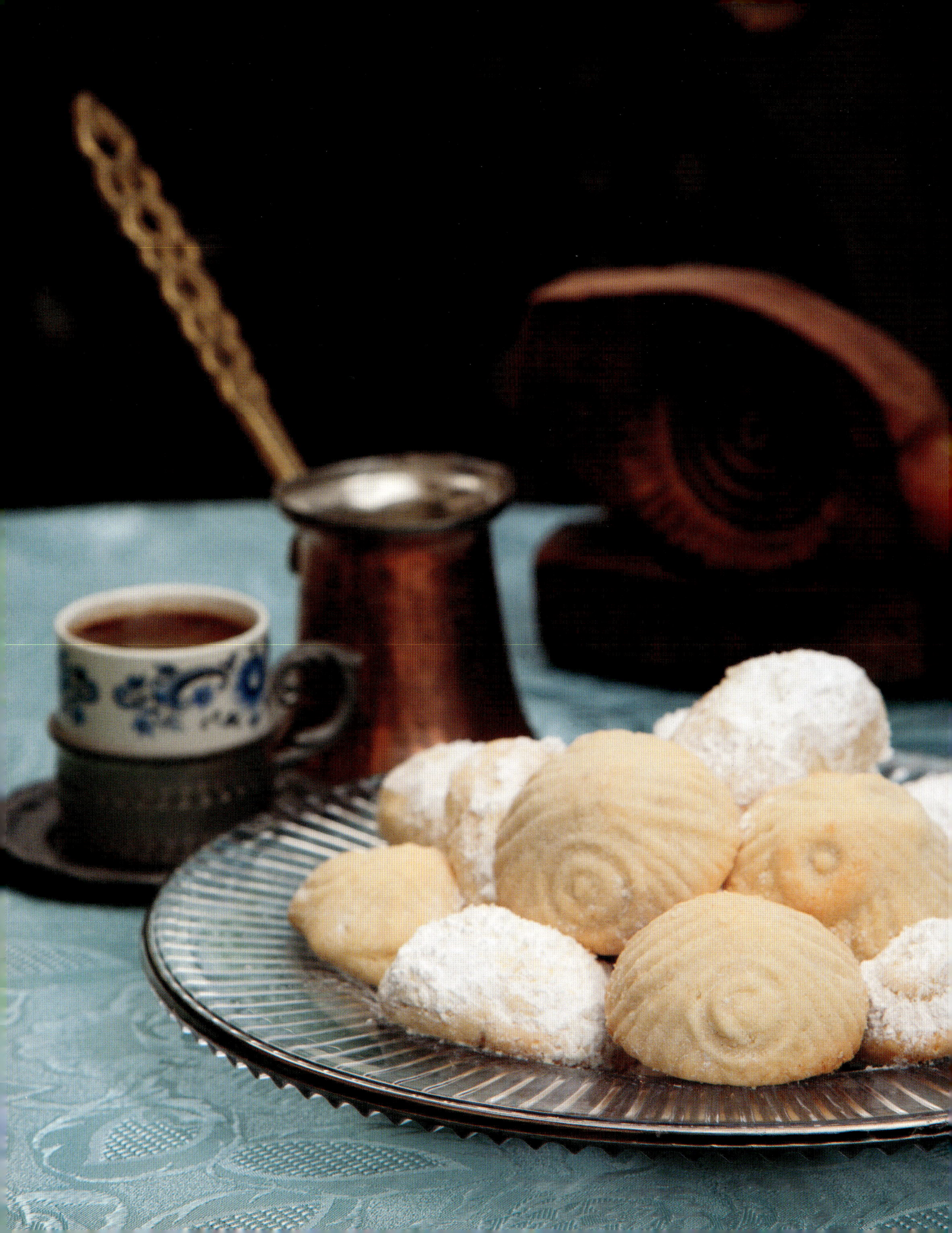

Semolina Biscuits with Walnuts
Ma'amoul

This is our Easter biscuit. When my mother and I made these biscuits she gave me the hard job of tasting one from the first batch as it came out of the oven (she was diabetic and did not eat sweets). I would eat it and tell her I needed to taste another one as the first one was too hot, and she would laugh and say, 'You have a sweet tooth! Go ahead and have another one.'

For the filling, mix all the ingredients together with your fingertips and set aside.

Place the semolina in a bowl, add the flour and butter and rub together with your fingertips for a good 10 minutes to combine thoroughly. Cover with plastic wrap and set aside for a minimum of 6 hours or overnight.

Preheat the oven to 180°C and line a baking tray with baking paper.

Add the rosewater to the biscuit mixture and rub the dough between your fingers until well combined. Divide into small balls about the size of a walnut and make a hole in the centre with your index finger. Place 1 teaspoon of the filling in the hole and close, sealing well so the filling won't escape while baking. Press firmly into a *ma'amoul* mould then gently tap out to remove and place on the baking tray, keeping each biscuit about 2cm apart. Continue with the remaining dough and filling.

Bake for 10 minutes, or until golden. Remove from the oven and leave to cool slightly. Dust with the icing sugar while still warm (use a sifter for this).

NOTE: The *ma'amoul* will keep in an air-tight container for up to 3 weeks.

Makes about 28

375g coarse semolina

250g self-raising flour

250g unsalted butter, melted

¼ cup rosewater

½ cup icing sugar

FILLING

150g walnuts, coarsely chopped

2 tablespoons white sugar

2 tablespoons orange blossom water

Date Biscuits

Sewa

375g coarse semolina

250g self-raising flour

250g unsalted butter, melted

¼ cup rosewater

1 teaspoon ground mahlab (available at Lebanese shops)

350g date paste (available at Lebanese shops)

Place the semolina in a bowl, add the sifted flour and melted butter and rub together with your fingertips for 10 minutes to combine thoroughly. Cover with plastic wrap and set aside for a minimum of 6 hours or overnight.

Preheat the oven to 180°C and line a baking tray with baking paper.

Rub the dough between your fingers and add the rosewater and the mahlab powder, continue mixing until well combined. Divide the mixture into small balls the size of a walnut, flatten each ball in the palm of your hand, add 1 teaspoon of the date paste and seal well. Press firmly into a *sewa* mould then gently tap out and place on the baking tray, keeping each biscuit about 2cm apart. Continue with the remaining dough and date paste.

Bake for 10 to 15 minutes, or until golden brown. Remove from the oven and leave to cool on a wire rack.

NOTE: The *sewa* will keep in an air-tight container for up 3 weeks.

Makes about 28

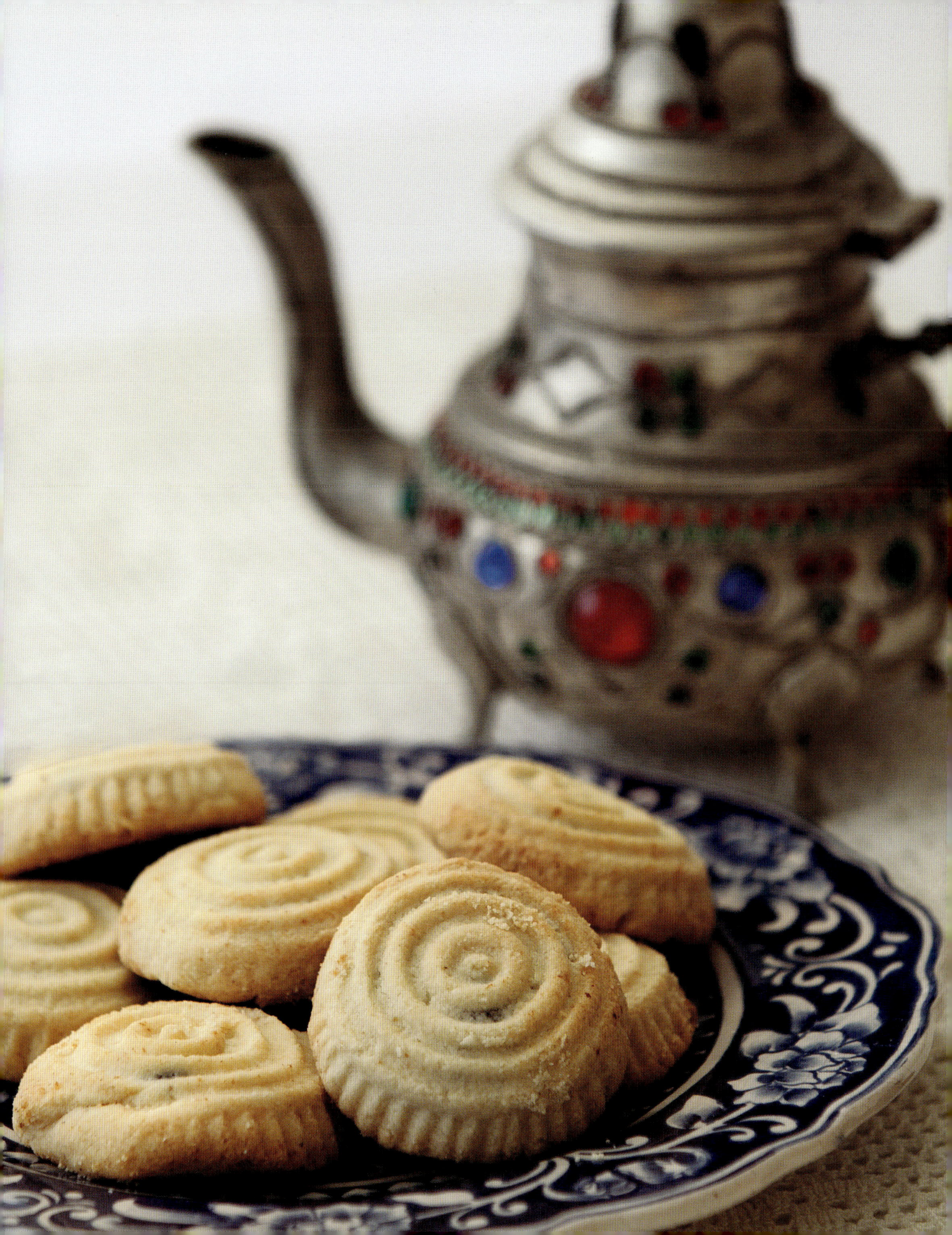

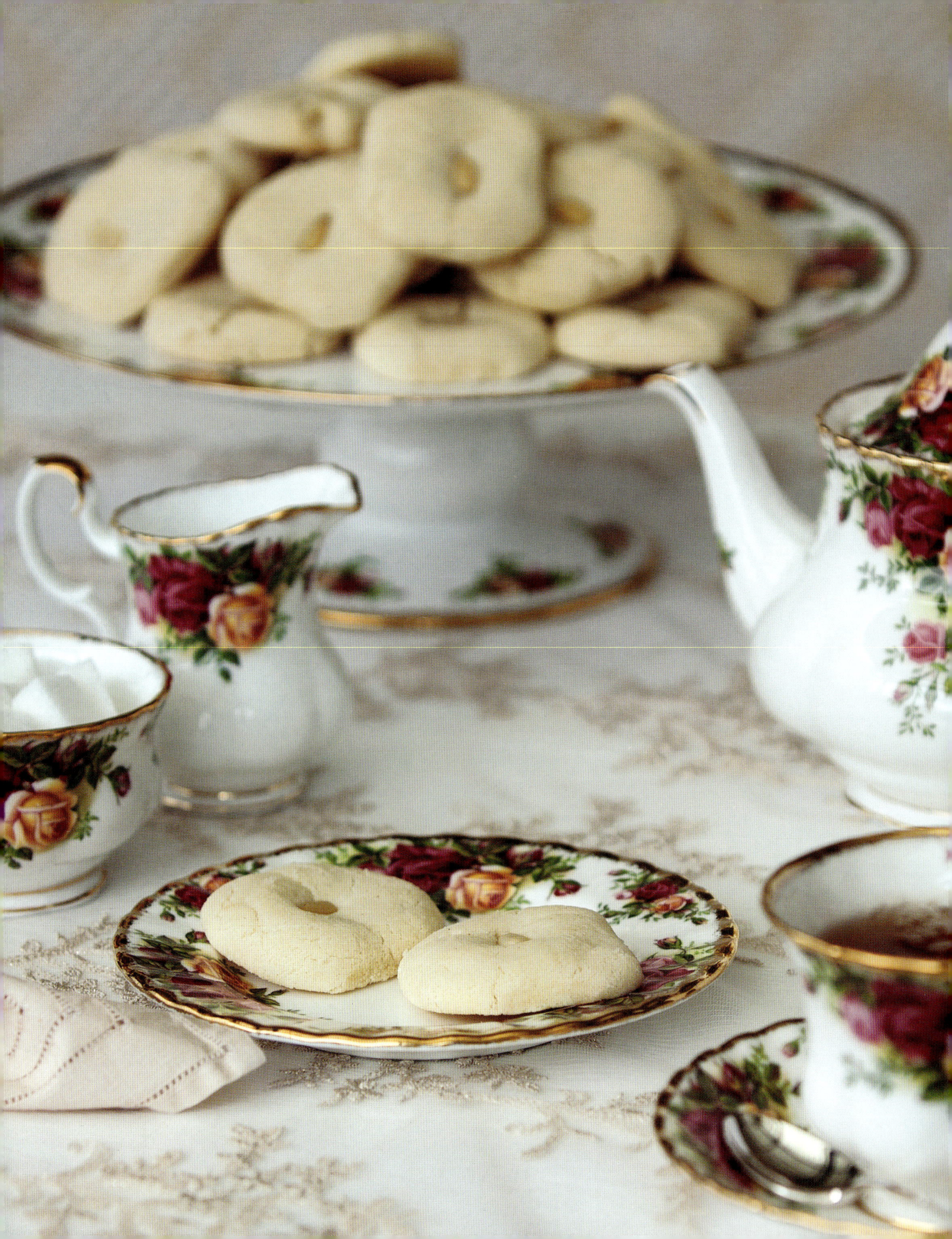

Shortbread Biscuits
G'raibeh

This is a very easy recipe although it can be hard to make it perfect every time. It really depends on the flour and butter you use.

Place the softened butter and the icing sugar in a bowl and beat with an electric mixer on low speed for 2 minutes, until the butter is fluffy. Add the flour and mix for a further 3 minutes, until combined. Place the bowl in the fridge to rest for 1 hour.

Preheat the oven to 140°C and line a baking tray with baking paper.

Divide the mixture into small balls the size of a walnut, flatten the top and press a pine nut or a halved almond in the centre of each and place on the baking tray, keeping each biscuit about 3cm apart. Continue until all the mixture is used.

Bake for 10–12 minutes, until lightly golden. Transfer to a wire rack, and when cold, pack into an air-tight container.

NOTE: The shortbread will keep for 3 weeks.

Makes 35–38

250g unsalted butter, softened

1½ cups icing sugar, sifted

2½ cups plain flour, sifted twice

¼ cup pine nuts or almonds, halved

Aniseed Biscuits

Kaak

½ cup sesame seeds

1 cup white sugar

1 cup vegetable oil

1 cup orange juice

1 tablespoon ground aniseed

½ teaspoon ground cinnamon

5 cups self-raising flour

This is our answer to the West's cookie jar. We always have kaak in the cookie jar. If you wish, you can make these with wholemeal flour.

Preheat the oven to 180°C and line a baking tray with baking paper. Spread the sesame seeds on a shallow plate.

Place the sugar, oil, orange juice, aniseed and cinnamon in a large bowl and mix well. Gradually add the sifted flour, kneading well to combine, to form a dough-like mixture.

Roll 1 heaped tablespoon of the dough between your hands or on a dusted surface to create a 10cm-long snake-like shape. Connect the ends together to make a ring, dip in the sesame seeds and place on the baking tray. Repeat until all the dough and sesame seeds are used, spacing the biscuits about 2cm apart.

Bake for 10 minutes, or until golden. Transfer to a wire rack when cold.

NOTE: The *kaak* will keep for at least 2 weeks in an air-tight container.

Makes 50–60

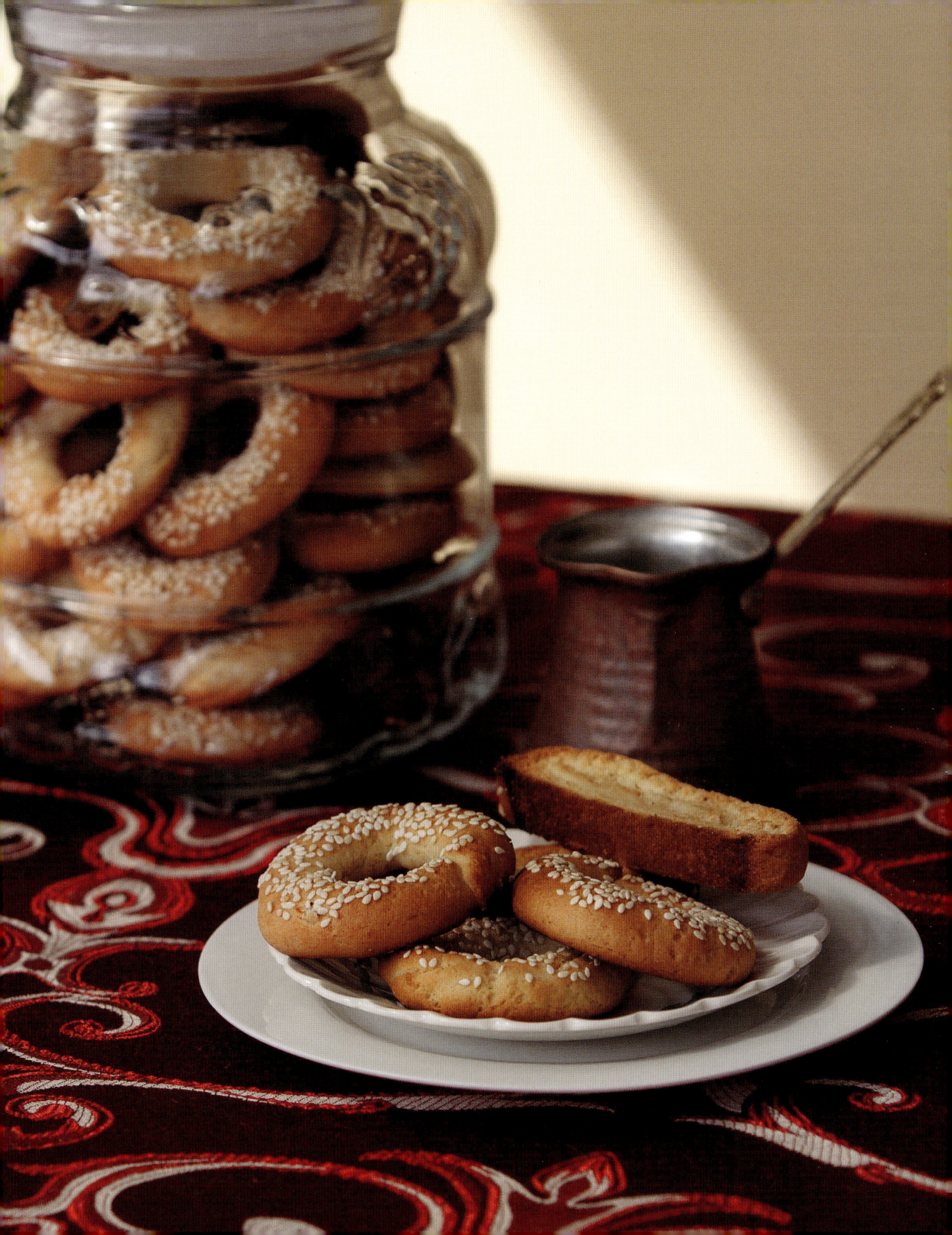

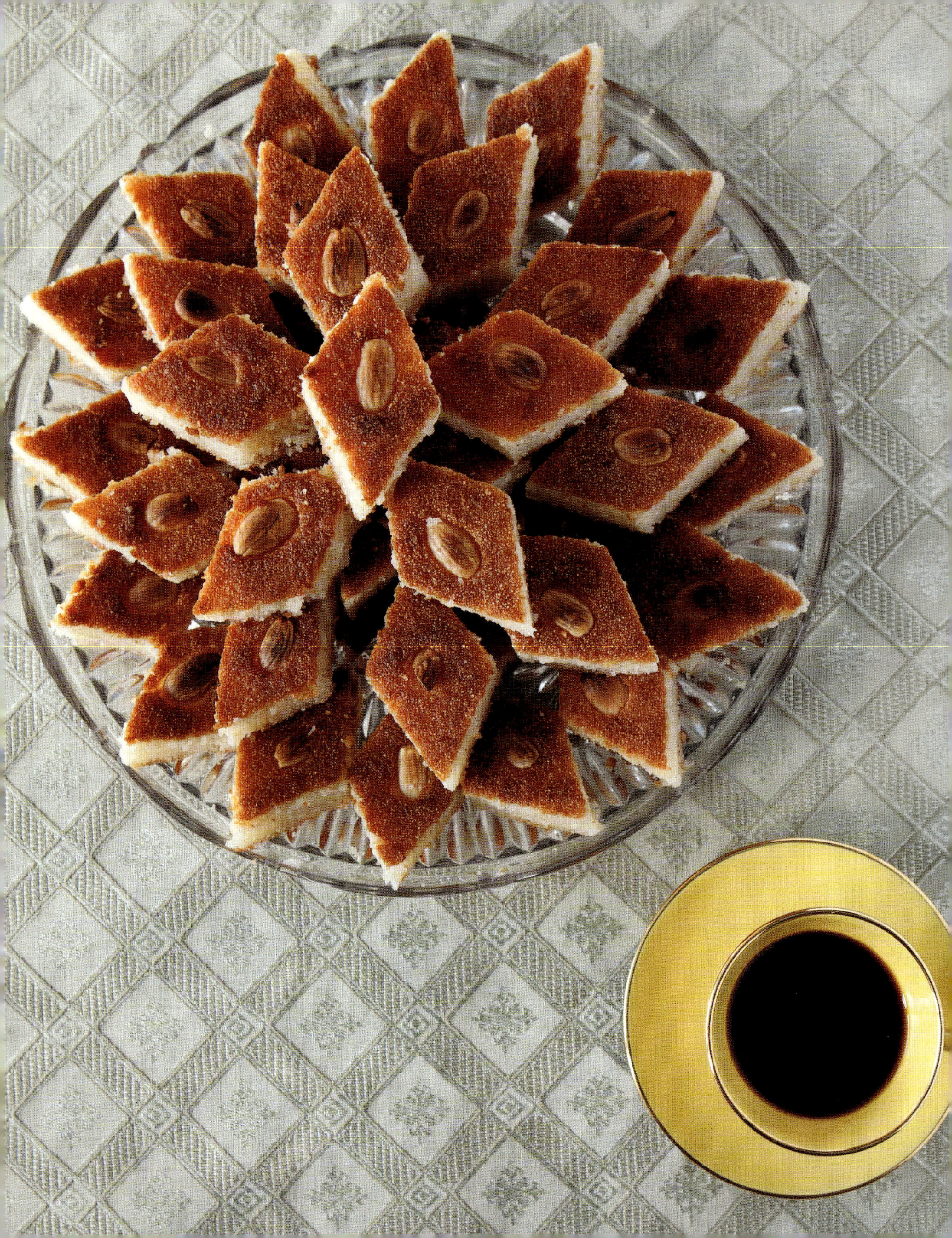

Semolina Slices

Nammoura

Nammoura is famous all over the Middle East. I remember in the summer the 'nammoura seller' used to come to the village with a large tray, about a metre in diameter, of nammoura balanced on his head and holding the stand under his arm. He walked from village to village, and the nammoura slices would melt in your mouth!

Grease a 30cm round or a 20cm x 30cm rectangular tray. Place the semolina, sugar, baking powder, coconut if using (I like the flavour) and milk in a large bowl and mix well. Pour the mixture into the prepared tray and smooth the surface. Set aside to rest for a minimum 8 hours or overnight.

Preheat the oven to 200°C.

Using a sharp knife to cut through the *nammoura*, make parallel cuts on the diagonal about 3cm apart, then cut on the diagonal in the opposite direction to create a diamond pattern. Place an almond half on the centre of each diamond. Bake for 40 minutes, or until golden brown.

Meanwhile, for the syrup, place the sugar and 1½ cups water in a saucepan and bring to the boil. Add the lemon juice, reduce the heat and simmer for 15 minutes. Remove from the heat, stir in the rosewater and keep warm.

Remove the *nammoura* from the oven and pour over the warm syrup. Leave to cool before serving.

NOTE: The *nammoura* will keep for 1 week in an air-tight container.

Makes about 50

---

5 cups coarse semolina

3 cups white sugar

1 teaspoon baking powder

1 cup desiccated coconut (optional)

2 cups milk

100g almonds, halved

SYRUP

3 cups white sugar

2 tablespoons lemon juice

2 tablespoons rosewater

Baklava
Backlawi

250g unsalted butter

375g packet filo pastry

300g cashews, finely chopped

100g walnuts, finely chopped

100g ground pistachios

SYRUP

2 cups white sugar

1 tablespoon lemon juice

2 tablespoons rosewater

Every country in the Middle East has a different version of backlawi.

For the syrup, place the sugar and 1 cup water in a saucepan and bring to the boil. Add the lemon juice, reduce the heat and simmer for 15 minutes. Remove from the heat, stir in the rosewater and keep warm.

Preheat the oven to 220°C and grease a 35cm x 20cm baking tray.

Melt the butter and keep warm for brushing. Cut the filo pastry to match the size of the baking dish (this will make it easy to manage). Layer 5 sheets of the pastry in the greased baking dish, brushing every second sheet with butter. Add the cashews and walnuts and cover with the leftover filo pastry, brushing every sheet with butter.

Using a sharp knife to cut through to the base, make parallel cuts on the diagonal about 4cm apart, then cut on the diagonal in the opposite way, about 3cm apart, to create a diamond pattern. Brush the top with any remaining butter.

Bake in the hot oven for 15 minutes then reduce the heat to 160°C and bake for another 30 minutes, or until golden brown. Remove from the oven and drizzle the hot syrup evenly over the top. When cool, decorate with the ground pistachios.

NOTE: The baklava will keep for up to 3 weeks in an air-tight container.

Makes about 25–30

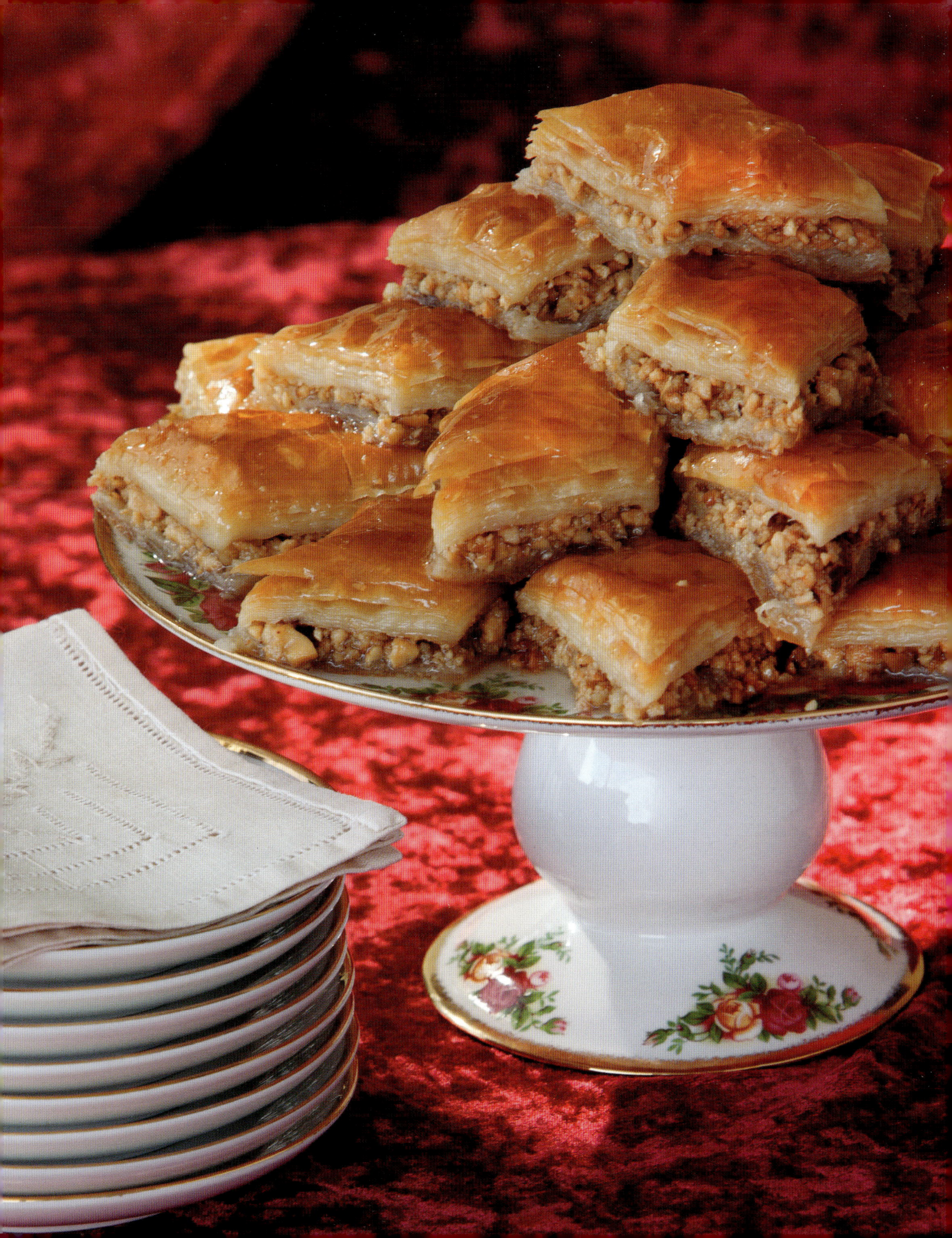

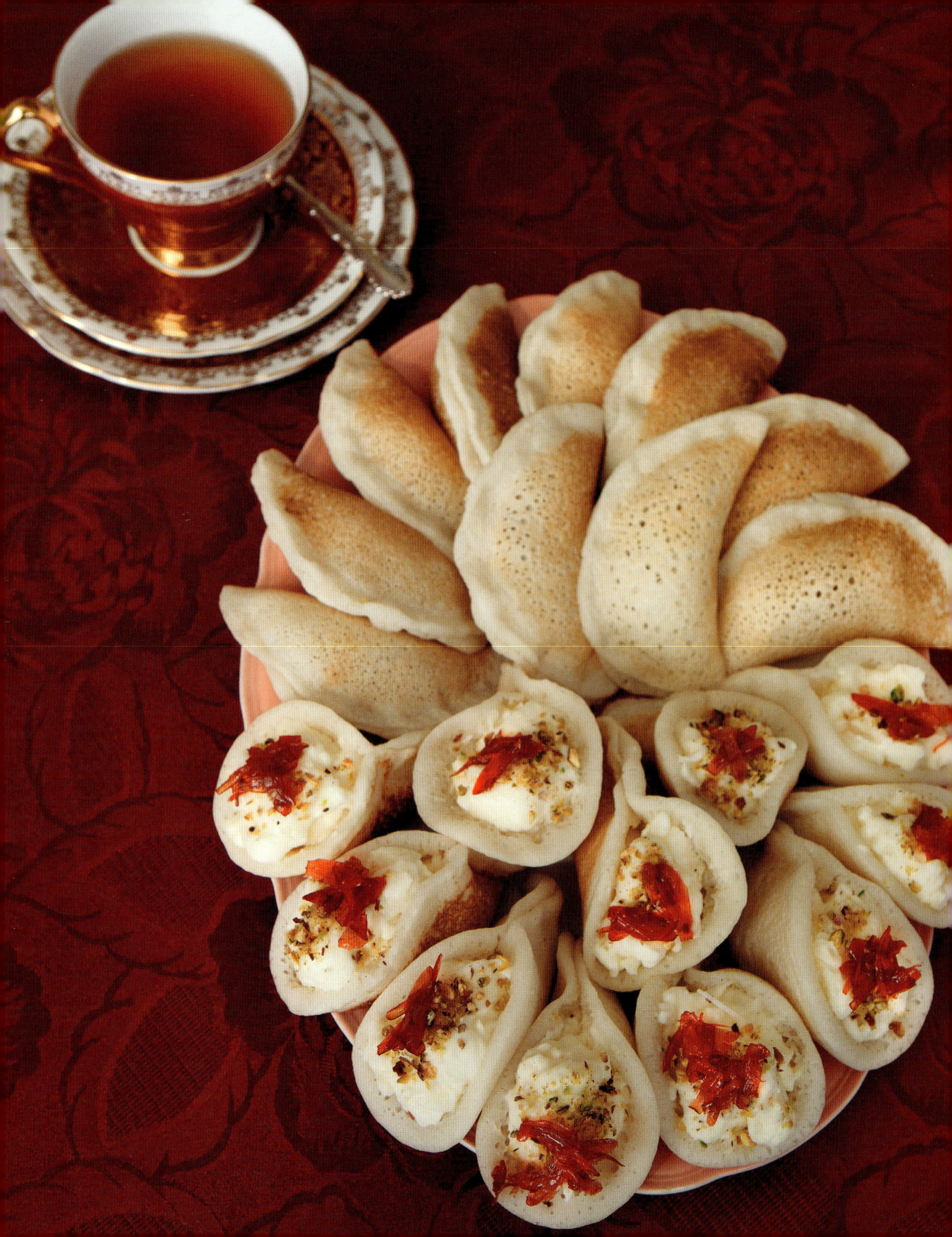

Pancakes with Walnuts or Cream
Katayef

For the syrup, place the sugar and 1 cup water in a saucepan and bring to the boil. Add the lemon juice, reduce the heat and simmer for 15 minutes. Remove from the heat and stir in the rosewater. Set aside to cool and refrigerate until ready to use.

For the pancakes, place the flour, semolina, sugar, yeast, baking powder, salt and 1¾ cups warm water in a large bowl and mix together with a whisk or electric hand mixer until you have a smooth batter. Cover with plastic wrap and set aside for 2 hours.

Meanwhile, for the cream filling, place all the ingredients in a saucepan over medium heat and whisk constantly until thick. Refrigerate before using. For the walnut filling, in a bowl, mix together all the ingredients and set aside.

After 2 hours, mix the pancake batter well, add ¼ cup water and mix again. Transfer to a pouring jug to make the batter easier to pour into the frying pan.

Heat a non-stick, heavy-based frying pan over medium heat. Pour in 2 tablespoons of the batter and cook for 2 minutes, or until the top becomes dry (do not turn over). Remove from the pan and place on a clean tea towel, cooked side down, to cool for a couple of minutes before filling with the walnut filling or the cream filling (if you delay the pancake will become dry). Repeat this step until all the batter is used.

To fill, hold a pancake in the palm of your hand, uncooked side up, add 1 tablespoon of the filling then fold the pancake over and press the edge firmly together to seal.

To serve, place the filled pancakes side by side on a serving dish, decorate with the pistachios and crystallised orange blossom and drizzle over the syrup.

NOTE: This recipe makes enough pancakes for either the walnut or cream filling. If you want both fillings then you will have to double the pancake quantity.

Makes 25–30

---

2 cups self-raising flour

½ cup fine semolina

3 tablespoons white sugar

1 teaspoon dried yeast

1 teaspoon baking powder

¼ teaspoon salt

¼ cup ground pistachios

crystallised orange blossom (available from Lebanese sweet shops)

CREAM FILLING

1½ cups milk

1 cup thickened cream

¼ cup cornflour

¼ cup plain flour

3 tablespoons white sugar

WALNUT FILLING

300g crushed walnuts

½ cup caster sugar

2 tablespoons rosewater

SYRUP

2 cups white sugar

1 tablespoon lemon juice

1 tablespoon rosewater

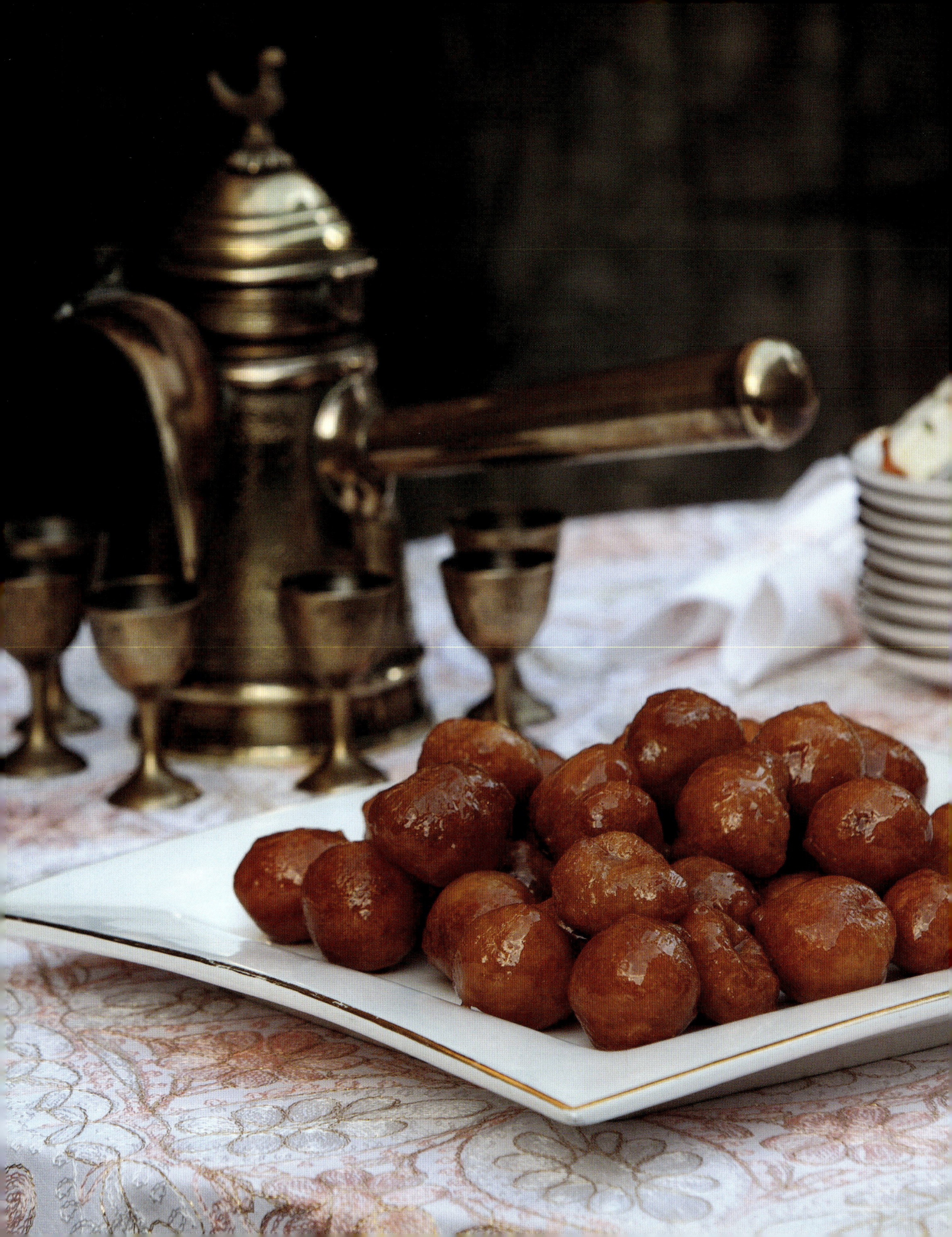

Doughnut Balls
Awamat

In Lebanon awamat were always prepared on the eve of Epiphany, which is 6 January. But now we prepare them quite often. They are so more-ish you can't stop at one.

Place all the dry ingredients in a large mixing bowl, mix well with a fork and add the water and the yoghurt. Using a hand mixer, beat at medium speed for 3–4 minutes until well combined. Cover with a tea towel and leave to rest in a warm place for 2 hours, until doubled in size.

Meanwhile, for the syrup, place the sugar and 1½ cups water in a saucepan and bring to the boil. Add the lemon juice, reduce the heat and simmer for 15 minutes. Remove from the heat, stir in the rosewater and keep warm.

In a deep-fryer or deep heavy-based saucepan, heat the oil to 320°C then reduce the temperature to medium. Drop a teaspoon of the dough mixture into the hot oil (you can do this in batches) and remove with a slotted spoon as soon as it turns golden. Drop into the warm syrup for 1–2 minutes, then remove and place on a serving dish.

Serve warm or cold.

NOTE: The *awamat* are best eaten on the day you make them.

Makes about 40–50

2 cups plain flour

¼ cup cornflour

1¼ teaspoons dried yeast

¼ teaspoon salt

¼ teaspoon ground cinnamon

1¼ cups warm water

¼ cup plain yogurt

1 litre corn oil, for deep-frying

SYRUP

3 cups white sugar

1 tablespoon lemon juice

1 tablespoon rosewater

Cream Slices
Ayesh el saraya

- 8 pieces French toast (available at most supermarkets)
- 3 cups milk
- 600ml cream
- 4 tablespoons white sugar
- ½ cup cornflour
- ½ cup plain flour
- 100g ground pistachios

SYRUP
- 2 cups white sugar
- 1 tablespoon lemon juice
- 2 tablespoons rosewater

For the syrup, place the sugar and 1½ cups water in a saucepan and bring to the boil. Add the lemon juice, reduce the heat and simmer for 15 minutes. Remove from the heat, stir in the rosewater and keep warm.

Place the French toast in a square or rectangular dish to cover the base, pour over half the quantity of the syrup and set aside.

Place the milk, cream, sugar, cornflour and plain flour in a saucepan and mix with a whisk or electric hand mixer until well combined. Place over medium heat and stir constantly with the whisk to prevent lumps forming, until thick (it should have a yoghurt-like consistency). Pour over the French toast and set aside to cool. Sprinkle with the ground pistachios and refrigerate for 2 hours.

Serve cold, with extra syrup if you wish.

Makes 8

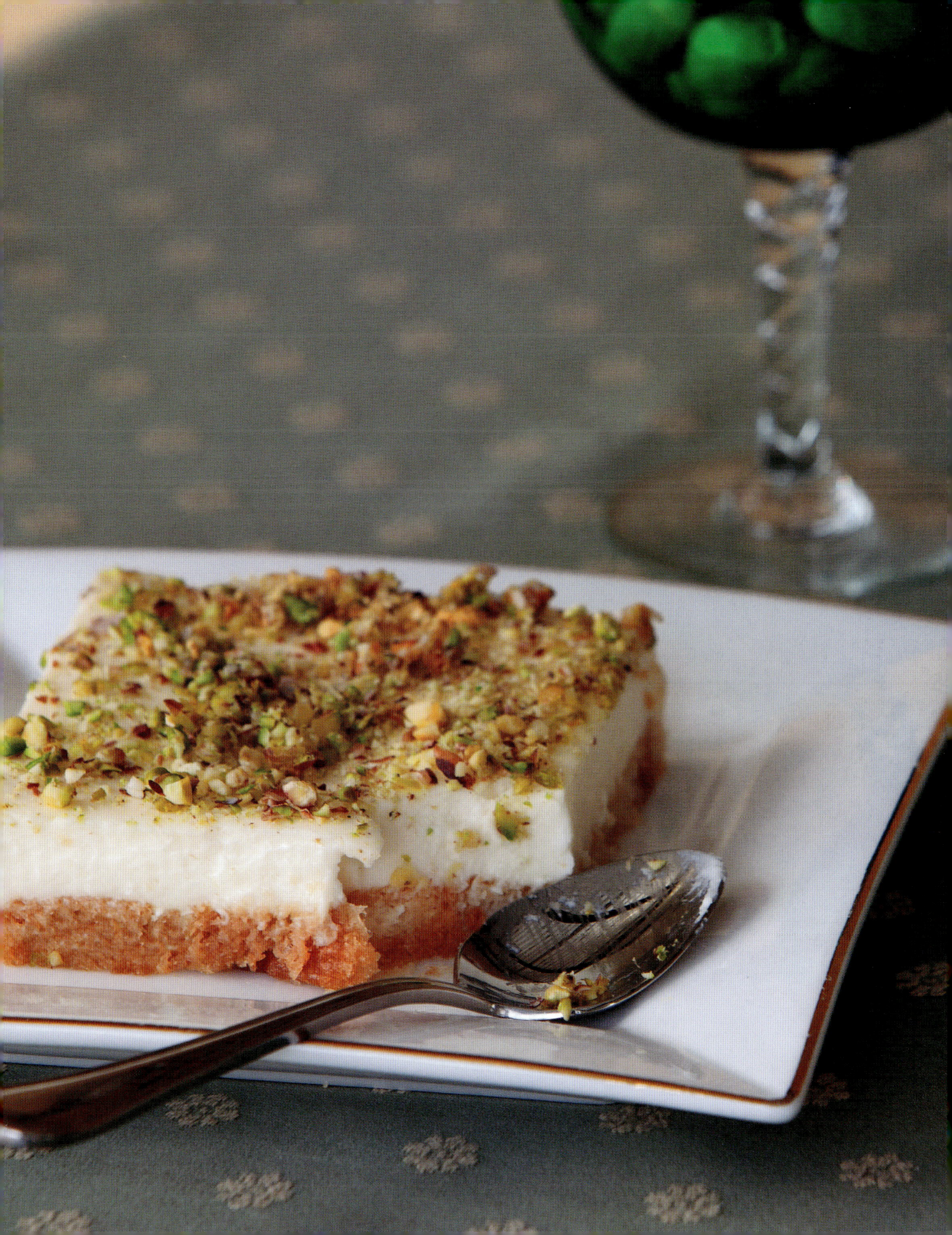

Sweet Cheese
Halawat el jibin

½ cup white sugar

500g mozzarella cheese or unsalted akkawi cheese (available at Lebanese shops), thinly sliced

1 cup fine semolina

¼ cup crushed pistachios

SYRUP

2 cups white sugar

1 tablespoon lemon juice

2 tablespoons rosewater

This is one of my favourite sweets. I have fond memories of walking to the Lebanese sweet shop and seeing the cheese draped across the window as it was made fresh daily.

Prepare the syrup before the sweet cheese. Place the sugar and 1 cup water in a saucepan and bring to the boil. Add the lemon juice, reduce the heat and simmer for 15 minutes. Remove from the heat, stir in the rosewater and set aside.

For the sweet cheese, place the sugar and 1½ cups water in a large saucepan and bring to the boil, stirring to dissolve the sugar. Add the cheese and stir constantly with a wooden spoon until the cheese has melted completely and become stringy. Reduce the heat and add the semolina gradually, stirring constantly for a few more minutes until combined. Remove from the heat.

On a flat clean surface, about 50cm x 50cm, pour out some of the warm syrup and spread well. Pour the cheese mixture over the syrup and use a rolling pin to spread and stretch the cheese, working quickly before it cools. Once cold, tear into small pieces and transfer to a tray. Cover and refrigerate for a minimum of 2 hours.

NOTE: You can serve the sweet cheese with just the syrup and crushed pistachios, or with ashta (Lebanese cream purchased from Lebanese sweet shops), or you can make the cream in the pancake recipe (see page 113). See over the page for step by step pictures of making Sweet Cheese.

Serves 8–10

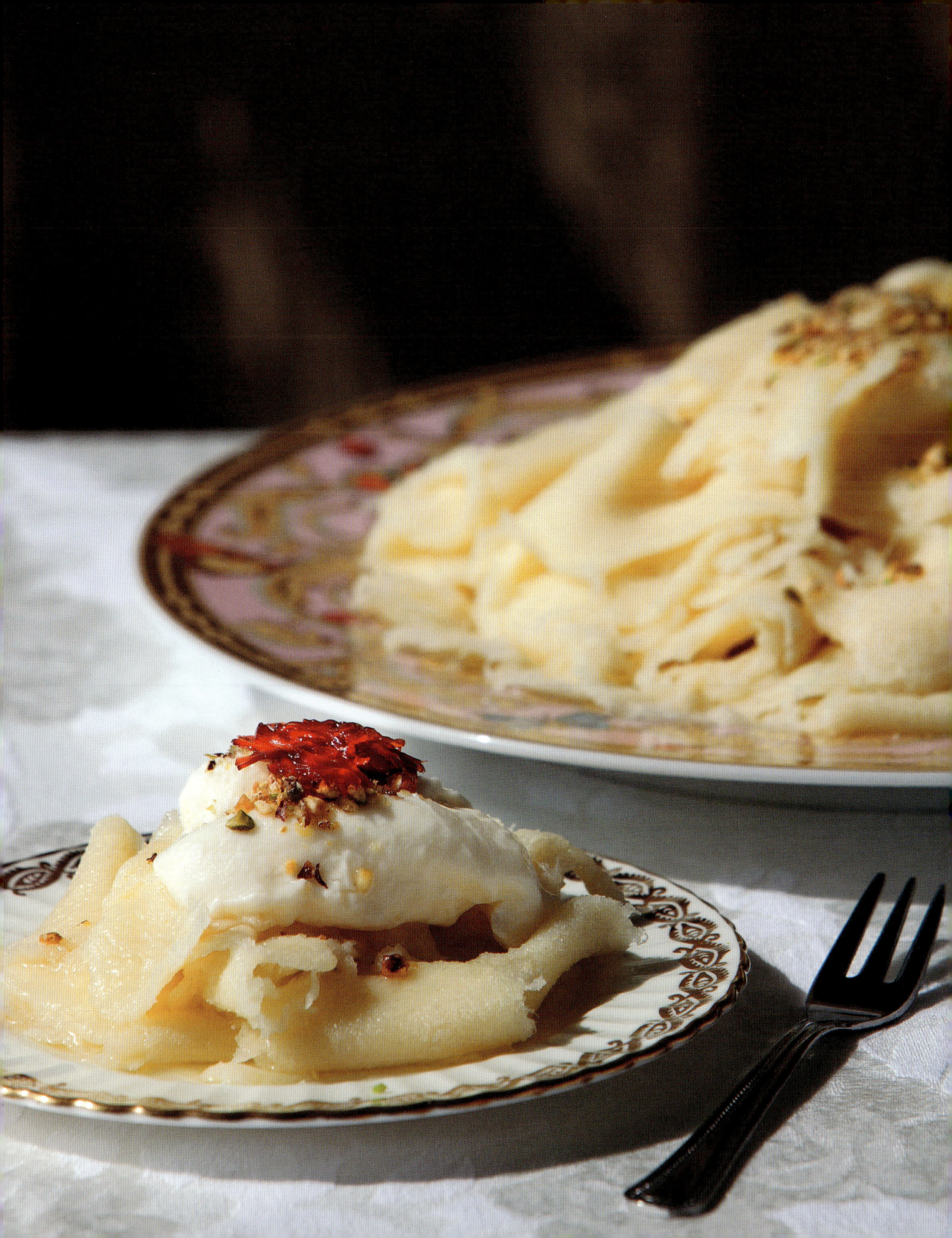

1

2

4

5

3

6

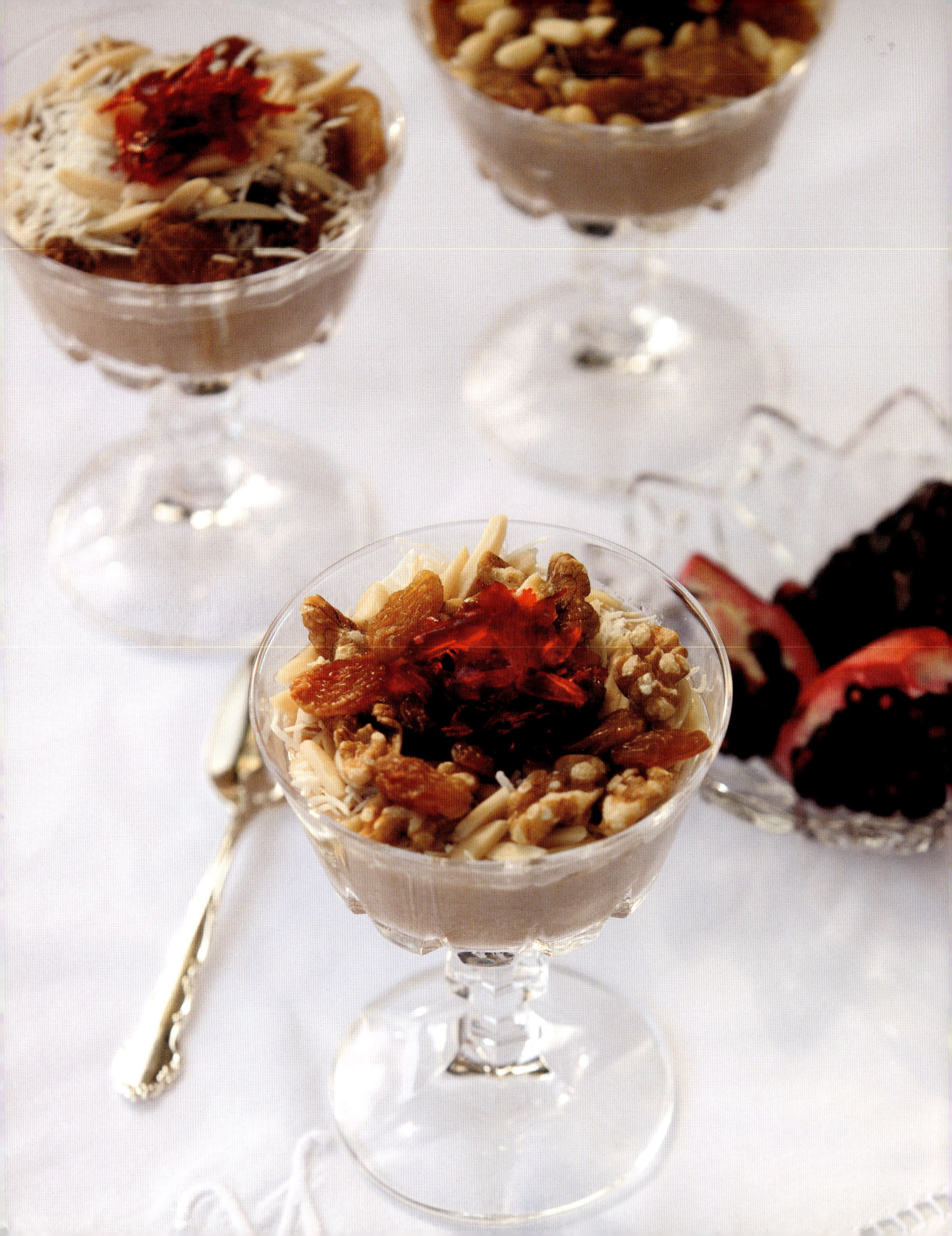

Lebanese Spicy Rice Pudding

Moghley

This traditional dish was made on the birth of a baby, including at Christmas when Jesus was born, and offered to family and friends.

Place 1.5 litres water in a saucepan and bring to the boil. Dissolve the rice flour in ½ cup water and add gradually to the pan. Reduce the heat and simmer for 30 minutes, stirring constantly to prevent it sticking to the pan. Add the sugar and all the spices and cook for a further 15 minutes, stirring constantly.

Pour into small serving bowls and set aside to cool. Decorate with the nuts, pine nuts, sultanas and coconut to serve.

NOTE: *Moghley* will keep in the fridge for 6 days.

Serves 6–8

100g rice flour

½ cup white sugar

½ tablespoon ground caraway

½ teaspoon ground aniseed

½ teaspoon ground cinnamon

¼ teaspoon fennel powder

½ cup walnuts, chopped

½ cup almonds, halved

¼ cup pine nuts

½ cup sultanas

½ cup shredded coconut

Sweet Wheat
Snainiyeh

1kg peeled wheat (available at Lebanese shops)

200g icing sugar

2 tablespoons rosewater

2 tablespoons ground cinnamon

DECORATIONS

200g walnuts

200g almonds, halved

100g sultanas or raisins

100g shredded coconut

300g sugar almonds

200g coloured chickpeas (available at Lebanese shops)

jelly babies

jellybeans

silver cachous

ribbons (optional)

Snainiyeh is prepared to celebrate a baby's first tooth. Grandparents would make this sweet and hand it out to family and friends. In return people would buy a small gift for the baby or give money.

Soak the wheat in 2 litres water overnight. The next day, drain and wash the wheat then place in a large saucepan with 2 litres water. Bring to the boil, then reduce the heat and simmer until the wheat is soft. Drain thoroughly, transfer to a bowl and add the icing sugar, rosewater and cinnamon. Combine well and set aside to cool.

The sweet wheat can be assembled on individual serving plates or in jars. If you are plating, divide the wheat across the plates and add all the decorations. If you are using jars, divide the wheat between the jars and then layer the decorations. Seal with the lid and tie on blue ribbons for boys or pink ribbons for girls. You could be extra creative and add a lollipop to the ribbons.

Makes 8

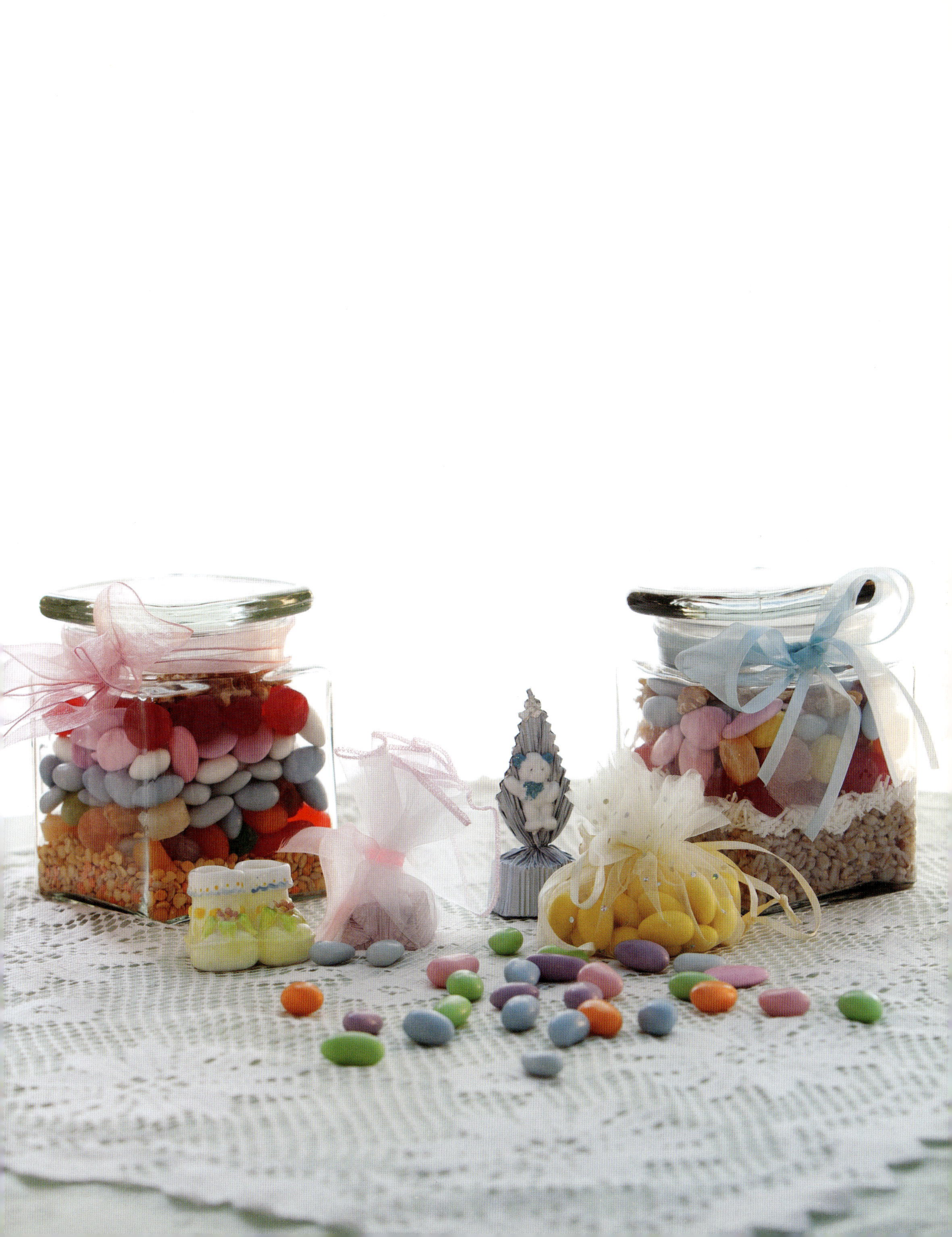

Fig Conserve
Mar'abba el tin

- 125g white sugar
- 2 tablespoons lemon juice
- 500g dried figs, stalks removed and thinly sliced
- ¾ cup roasted almonds, halved
- 1 teaspoon aniseed powder or mastiqua powder (available at Lebanese shops)

Place the sugar and 150ml water in a saucepan and bring to the boil. Add the lemon juice and boil for 1–2 minutes, then add the sliced figs and stir. Reduce the heat to low and cook for about 20 minutes, stirring regularly to prevent the mixture sticking to the pan. Add the almonds and the aniseed or mastiqua powder and cook for a further 10 minutes.

Remove from the heat and transfer to the sterilised jars while still warm. Leave to cool before sealing.

NOTE: The conserve can be stored for up to 6 months.

Makes about 2 x 350g jars

Acknowledgements

I would like to thank my children and their families for working so closely with me while on my journey scribing all the memories of my childhood cooking experiences with my mother and grandmother. Without their love, help and support writing this cookbook wouldn't have been possible.

A special thanks to my nieces Sharlene and Evy Mourched for taking time out from their university break to help with the photo shoot. To Robin Brook for sharing some of her beautiful antique plates, and to my dear friends Georgette Katrib and Mel Kessanis for their help with testing the recipes and enjoying the experience with me.

A special thank you to Wendy McDougall for taking such beautiful photos (you are such a perfectionist), to Kerry Klinner for her design skills and making my book look so beautiful and to my editor, Glenda Downing, for making sense of my writing.

Lastly, but not least, a big thank you to Victoria Jefferys for making the production of this cookbook such a wonderful experience. You and Wendy were an absolute pleasure to work with. Thank you for your encouragement, support and all the laughs.

First published in Australia in 2012 by WriteLight Pty Ltd
for Sue Dahman
1 Tallowwood Avenue, Lugarno NSW 2210
Ph: +61425306136
www.taytaslebanesekitchen.com.au

© text Sue Dahman
© photographs Wendy McDougall
© photograph on pages 4–5 Paul Burrows

This book is copyright. No part may be reproduced by any process without permission from the Copyright Owners.

National Library of Australia Cataloguing-in-Publication data
Dahman, Sue.
   Tayta's Lebanese kitchen / Sue Dahman.
   780980687873 (pbk.)
   Cooking, Lebanese.
Dewey Number: 641.595692
ISBN 978-0-9806878-7-3

Distributed by Woodslane Pty Ltd
10 Apollo Street Warriewood NSW 2102 Australia
Ph: +612 8445 2300
Fax: +612 9997 5850

Photography: Wendy McDougall
Editor: Glenda Downing
Design: Kerry Klinner, Megacity Design
Production: Victoria Jefferys
Pre-press: Graphic Print Group
Printed in China by Everbest Printing Co.